# Paradise Partners v. D.J. Diamond

**Case File**
**Trial Materials**

# PARADISE PARTNERS V. D.J. DIAMOND

**Case File**
**Trial Materials**

**Carl W. Chamberlin**
Lead Appellate Court Attorney
California Court of Appeal

**The Hon. Marian F. Gaston**
San Diego Superior Court Judge

NITA®
NATIONAL INSTITUTE FOR TRIAL ADVOCACY

Address inquiries to:
Reprint Permission
National Institute for Trial Advocacy
325 W. South Boulder Rd., Ste. 1
Louisville, CO 80027-1130
Phone: (800) 225-6482
E-mail: publications@nita.org

ISBN 979-8-88669-093-4
FBA 2093
eISBN 979-8-88669-094-1
eFBA 2094

ASPEN PUBLISHING

Official co-publisher of NITA.
aspenpublishing.com/NITA

# Contents

# Acknowledgments

The authors would like to thank Carolyn Meyer for being our *Gossip Grrrl.* Carolyn, you did a great job!

The authors would also like to thank Brady Carpenter, Elaine Lehnert, and everyone else at Ankura for their excellent work on the financial analysis presented in this case file.

# Introduction

This case involves a business dispute between Paradise Partners (Paradise), a not-for-profit organization dedicated to improving the lives of disadvantaged youth, and musical sensation D.J. Diamond (Diamond). Paradise had contracted with Diamond to perform a charity concert. Paradise anticipated raising millions of dollars to benefit its annual summer camp for foster and low-income children.

Diamond did not perform. As a result, the concert was canceled, and Paradise claims it had no funds to host its annual summer camp and may not be able to host one again. In the aftermath of the concert's cancellation, staff at Paradise manipulated a video that Diamond had made announcing the charity concert, without Diamond's permission, to create a deepfake video of Diamond requesting donations for Paradise.

Paradise has sued, alleging breach of contract. Diamond admits not performing but denies a breach, claiming that the contract's cancellation clause permitted the cancellation. The parties dispute the meaning of the clause and the reason for Diamond's refusal to perform.

Diamond has countersued Paradise, alleging the deepfake was copyright infringement.* Paradise has defended, alleging affirmative defenses including fair use of Diamond's copyrighted material.

There are four lay witnesses:

- Payton Plaze, founder of Paradise Partners
- Pat Paw, Assistant Director of Fundraising at Paradise Partners
- D.J. Diamond, celebrity performer
- Dakota "Doomsday" Dyer, manager and agent for D.J. Diamond

Each side has retained an expert on damages:

- Parker Emory Pearce, PhD, for the plaintiff
- Professor Dylan E. Donahue for the defense

* Some programs may not utilize the countersuit. Confirm with your instructor or program director whether you will be addressing this issue.

# Instructions

**Please read the following carefully.**

This file may be used:

- on the issue of Diamond's liability only;
- on the issues of Diamond's liability and damages;
- on the issue of Paradise's liability on the counterclaim;
- on the issues of Diamond's liability and Paradise's liability on the counterclaim; or
- on the issues of Diamond's liability, Paradise's liability on the counterclaim, and damages.

The file is suitable for training in deposition, trial, and negotiation skills. Your instructor will indicate which issues and skills pertain to your program or course.

The applicable law is contained in the jury instructions set forth at the end of this case file.

It is not necessary to study in detail the Exhibit 5 letter from Concerts-R-Us. Although it constitutes a contract between Concerts-R-Us and Paradise Partners, much of it consists of background information that is not directly germane to the case but is included for those who are interested.

All years in these materials are stated in the following form:

1) YR-0 indicates the actual year in which the case is being tried (i.e., the present year);

2) YR-1 indicates the next preceding year (please use the actual year);

3) YR-2 indicates the second preceding year (please use the actual year), etc.

To avoid logistical issues with dates, assume February 12 is a Sunday, no matter when it falls in the actual year. A fixed calendar for YR-1 and YR-2 is provided to assist with keeping the days accurate. To avoid logistical issues with dates of deposition testimony, signatures and court reporter certifications have been omitted.

Copies of the exhibits are available online at:

https://bit.ly/43axcZr
Password: Paradise1

# Stipulations

1. All exhibits are true and correct copies of the original documents.
2. All pretrial motions for temporary injunctions were denied.
3. Regard transcriptions of any audio or video materials as the true and accurate version of those materials.
4. All depositions were properly attested, signed, and certified.
5. Feb. 12, YR-1, fell on a Sunday.
6. Operating costs for Paradise Partners have been reviewed by accountants for D.J. Diamond and are acceptable expenses for a nonprofit organization of its size.
7. At trial, the court rules that Paw's diary is inadmissible.
8. Yummy refused to communicate with the parties regarding this litigation and is outside the court's jurisdiction.

# Timeline

| | |
|---|---|
| YR-4 | Plaze founds Paradise Partners. |
| February YR-2 | Plaze hires Paw as assistant fundraiser. |
| November YR-2 | Idea of benefit concert surfaces. |
| November 28, YR-2 | Paw texts asking Diamond to perform concert; Diamond says yes. |
| November 28, YR-2 | Paw calls Concerts-R-Us. |
| November 29, YR-2 | Paw speaks with Dyer by phone. |
| November 30, YR-2 | Paw receives and signs concert contract from Dyer, setting concert for February 12, YR-1. |
| December 1, YR-2 | Dyer contacts Concerts-R-Us with Diamond's needs, provides a copy of the concert contract, approves Nita Amphitheater as venue. |
| December 2, YR-2 | Concerts-R-Us letter/contract to Paw; Paw signs. |
| Dec. YR-2–Feb. YR-1 | Concerts-R-Us obtains venue, staff, etc. |
| December 9, YR-2 | Diamond/Dyer create marketing video for concert. |
| December 10, YR-2 | Dyer provides marketing video to Paradise/Concerts-R-Us. |
| December 11, YR-2 | Concerts-R-Us releases marketing video. |
| January 2, YR-1 | Concert tickets go on sale and sell out within minutes. |
| February 10, YR-1 | Dyer texts Paw that Diamond cannot perform. |
| February 11, YR-1 | Paradise sends out announcement canceling concert. |
| February 12, YR-1 | Date for concert and Super Bowl Sunday; Plaze sends letter to Dyer seeking resolution of dispute/compensation. |
| February 13, YR-1 | Concerts-R-Us letter to Paw stating $34K owed and calculating over $2.5M lost revenue from cancellation. |
| February 19, YR-1 | Dyer responds to Plaze's letter. |
| February 22, YR-1 | Plaze receives Dyer's letter. |
| March 13, YR-1 | Paradise cancels camp reservation to avoid nonrefundable camp fees. |
| March 14, YR-1 | Paradise files lawsuit against Diamond; Plaze issues press release (Diamond is served on March 15). |

| | |
|---|---|
| March 20, YR-1 | Plaze uses the marketing video and an AI app to create a deepfake video of Diamond soliciting donations for Paradise. |
| March 24, YR-1 | Paradise releases the deepfake video that Plaze created. |
| March 25, YR-1 | Dyer and Diamond see deepfake video. |
| April 4, YR-1 | Diamond answers complaint and files counterclaim. |
| April 24, YR-1 | Paradise answers counterclaim. |
| May 31, YR-1 | Dyer receives certificate of copyright registration from Copyright Office. |
| June YR-1 | Planned camp date (four one-week sessions). |

# CALENDAR

## YR-2

### JANUARY

| S | M | T | W | T | F | S |
|---|---|---|---|---|---|---|
| | | | | | | 1 |
| 2 | 3 | 4 | 5 | 6 | 7 | 8 |
| 9 | 10 | 11 | 12 | 13 | 14 | 15 |
| 16 | 17 | 18 | 19 | 20 | 21 | 22 |
| 23 | 24 | 25 | 26 | 27 | 28 | 29 |
| 30 | 31 | | | | | |

### FEBRUARY

| S | M | T | W | T | F | S |
|---|---|---|---|---|---|---|
| | | 1 | 2 | 3 | 4 | 5 |
| 6 | 7 | 8 | 9 | 10 | 11 | 12 |
| 13 | 14 | 15 | 16 | 17 | 18 | 19 |
| 20 | 21 | 22 | 23 | 24 | 25 | 26 |
| 27 | 28 | | | | | |

### MARCH

| S | M | T | W | T | F | S |
|---|---|---|---|---|---|---|
| | | 1 | 2 | 3 | 4 | 5 |
| 6 | 7 | 8 | 9 | 10 | 11 | 12 |
| 13 | 14 | 15 | 16 | 17 | 18 | 19 |
| 20 | 21 | 22 | 23 | 24 | 25 | 26 |
| 27 | 28 | 29 | 30 | 31 | | |

### APRIL

| S | M | T | W | T | F | S |
|---|---|---|---|---|---|---|
| | | | | | 1 | 2 |
| 3 | 4 | 5 | 6 | 7 | 8 | 9 |
| 10 | 11 | 12 | 13 | 14 | 15 | 16 |
| 17 | 18 | 19 | 20 | 21 | 22 | 23 |
| 24 | 25 | 26 | 27 | 28 | 29 | 30 |

### MAY

| S | M | T | W | T | F | S |
|---|---|---|---|---|---|---|
| 1 | 2 | 3 | 4 | 5 | 6 | 7 |
| 8 | 9 | 10 | 11 | 12 | 13 | 14 |
| 15 | 16 | 17 | 18 | 19 | 20 | 21 |
| 22 | 23 | 24 | 25 | 26 | 27 | 28 |
| 29 | 30 | 31 | | | | |

### JUNE

| S | M | T | W | T | F | S |
|---|---|---|---|---|---|---|
| | | | 1 | 2 | 3 | 4 |
| 5 | 6 | 7 | 8 | 9 | 10 | 11 |
| 12 | 13 | 14 | 15 | 16 | 17 | 18 |
| 19 | 20 | 21 | 22 | 23 | 24 | 25 |
| 26 | 27 | 28 | 29 | 30 | | |

### JULY

| S | M | T | W | T | F | S |
|---|---|---|---|---|---|---|
| | | | | | 1 | 2 |
| 3 | 4 | 5 | 6 | 7 | 8 | 9 |
| 10 | 11 | 12 | 13 | 14 | 15 | 16 |
| 17 | 18 | 19 | 20 | 21 | 22 | 23 |
| 24 | 25 | 26 | 27 | 28 | 29 | 30 |
| 31 | | | | | | |

### AUGUST

| S | M | T | W | T | F | S |
|---|---|---|---|---|---|---|
| | 1 | 2 | 3 | 4 | 5 | 6 |
| 7 | 8 | 9 | 10 | 11 | 12 | 13 |
| 14 | 15 | 16 | 17 | 18 | 19 | 20 |
| 21 | 22 | 23 | 24 | 25 | 26 | 27 |
| 28 | 29 | 30 | 31 | | | |

### SEPTEMBER

| S | M | T | W | T | F | S |
|---|---|---|---|---|---|---|
| | | | | 1 | 2 | 3 |
| 4 | 5 | 6 | 7 | 8 | 9 | 10 |
| 11 | 12 | 13 | 14 | 15 | 16 | 17 |
| 18 | 19 | 20 | 21 | 22 | 23 | 24 |
| 25 | 26 | 27 | 28 | 29 | 30 | |

### OCTOBER

| S | M | T | W | T | F | S |
|---|---|---|---|---|---|---|
| | | | | | | 1 |
| 2 | 3 | 4 | 5 | 6 | 7 | 8 |
| 9 | 10 | 11 | 12 | 13 | 14 | 15 |
| 16 | 17 | 18 | 19 | 20 | 21 | 22 |
| 23 | 24 | 25 | 26 | 27 | 28 | 29 |
| 30 | 31 | | | | | |

### NOVEMBER

| S | M | T | W | T | F | S |
|---|---|---|---|---|---|---|
| | | 1 | 2 | 3 | 4 | 5 |
| 6 | 7 | 8 | 9 | 10 | 11 | 12 |
| 13 | 14 | 15 | 16 | 17 | 18 | 19 |
| 20 | 21 | 22 | 23 | 24 | 25 | 26 |
| 27 | 28 | 29 | 30 | | | |

### DECEMBER

| S | M | T | W | T | F | S |
|---|---|---|---|---|---|---|
| | | | | 1 | 2 | 3 |
| 4 | 5 | 6 | 7 | 8 | 9 | 10 |
| 11 | 12 | 13 | 14 | 15 | 16 | 17 |
| 18 | 19 | 20 | 21 | 22 | 23 | 24 |
| 25 | 26 | 27 | 28 | 29 | 30 | 31 |

## YR-1

### JANUARY

| S | M | T | W | T | F | S |
|---|---|---|---|---|---|---|
| 1 | 2 | 3 | 4 | 5 | 6 | 7 |
| 8 | 9 | 10 | 11 | 12 | 13 | 14 |
| 15 | 16 | 17 | 18 | 19 | 20 | 21 |
| 22 | 23 | 24 | 25 | 26 | 27 | 28 |
| 29 | 30 | 31 | | | | |

### FEBRUARY

| S | M | T | W | T | F | S |
|---|---|---|---|---|---|---|
| | | | 1 | 2 | 3 | 4 |
| 5 | 6 | 7 | 8 | 9 | 10 | 11 |
| 12 | 13 | 14 | 15 | 16 | 17 | 18 |
| 19 | 20 | 21 | 22 | 23 | 24 | 25 |
| 26 | 27 | 28 | | | | |

### MARCH

| S | M | T | W | T | F | S |
|---|---|---|---|---|---|---|
| | | | 1 | 2 | 3 | 4 |
| 5 | 6 | 7 | 8 | 9 | 10 | 11 |
| 12 | 13 | 14 | 15 | 16 | 17 | 18 |
| 19 | 20 | 21 | 22 | 23 | 24 | 25 |
| 26 | 27 | 28 | 29 | 30 | 31 | |

### APRIL

| S | M | T | W | T | F | S |
|---|---|---|---|---|---|---|
| | | | | | | 1 |
| 2 | 3 | 4 | 5 | 6 | 7 | 8 |
| 9 | 10 | 11 | 12 | 13 | 14 | 15 |
| 16 | 17 | 18 | 19 | 20 | 21 | 22 |
| 23 | 24 | 25 | 26 | 27 | 28 | 29 |
| 30 | | | | | | |

### MAY

| S | M | T | W | T | F | S |
|---|---|---|---|---|---|---|
| | 1 | 2 | 3 | 4 | 5 | 6 |
| 7 | 8 | 9 | 10 | 11 | 12 | 13 |
| 14 | 15 | 16 | 17 | 18 | 19 | 20 |
| 21 | 22 | 23 | 24 | 25 | 26 | 27 |
| 28 | 29 | 30 | 31 | | | |

### JUNE

| S | M | T | W | T | F | S |
|---|---|---|---|---|---|---|
| | | | | 1 | 2 | 3 |
| 4 | 5 | 6 | 7 | 8 | 9 | 10 |
| 11 | 12 | 13 | 14 | 15 | 16 | 17 |
| 18 | 19 | 20 | 21 | 22 | 23 | 24 |
| 25 | 26 | 27 | 28 | 29 | 30 | |

### JULY

| S | M | T | W | T | F | S |
|---|---|---|---|---|---|---|
| | | | | | | 1 |
| 2 | 3 | 4 | 5 | 6 | 7 | 8 |
| 9 | 10 | 11 | 12 | 13 | 14 | 15 |
| 16 | 17 | 18 | 19 | 20 | 21 | 22 |
| 23 | 24 | 25 | 26 | 27 | 28 | 29 |
| 30 | 31 | | | | | |

### AUGUST

| S | M | T | W | T | F | S |
|---|---|---|---|---|---|---|
| | | 1 | 2 | 3 | 4 | 5 |
| 6 | 7 | 8 | 9 | 10 | 11 | 12 |
| 13 | 14 | 15 | 16 | 17 | 18 | 19 |
| 20 | 21 | 22 | 23 | 24 | 25 | 26 |
| 27 | 28 | 29 | 30 | 31 | | |

### SEPTEMBER

| S | M | T | W | T | F | S |
|---|---|---|---|---|---|---|
| | | | | | 1 | 2 |
| 3 | 4 | 5 | 6 | 7 | 8 | 9 |
| 10 | 11 | 12 | 13 | 14 | 15 | 16 |
| 17 | 18 | 19 | 20 | 21 | 22 | 23 |
| 24 | 25 | 26 | 27 | 28 | 29 | 30 |

### OCTOBER

| S | M | T | W | T | F | S |
|---|---|---|---|---|---|---|
| 1 | 2 | 3 | 4 | 5 | 6 | 7 |
| 8 | 9 | 10 | 11 | 12 | 13 | 14 |
| 15 | 16 | 17 | 18 | 19 | 20 | 21 |
| 22 | 23 | 24 | 25 | 26 | 27 | 28 |
| 29 | 30 | 31 | | | | |

### NOVEMBER

| S | M | T | W | T | F | S |
|---|---|---|---|---|---|---|
| | | | 1 | 2 | 3 | 4 |
| 5 | 6 | 7 | 8 | 9 | 10 | 11 |
| 12 | 13 | 14 | 15 | 16 | 17 | 18 |
| 19 | 20 | 21 | 22 | 23 | 24 | 25 |
| 26 | 27 | 28 | 29 | 30 | | |

### DECEMBER

| S | M | T | W | T | F | S |
|---|---|---|---|---|---|---|
| | | | | | 1 | 2 |
| 3 | 4 | 5 | 6 | 7 | 8 | 9 |
| 10 | 11 | 12 | 13 | 14 | 15 | 16 |
| 17 | 18 | 19 | 20 | 21 | 22 | 23 |
| 24 | 25 | 26 | 27 | 28 | 29 | 30 |
| 31 | | | | | | |

# Pleadings

**UNITED STATES DISTRICT COURT**
**NORTHERN DISTRICT OF NITA**

| | |
|---|---|
| PARADISE PARTNERS,<br>Plaintiff,<br><br>v.<br><br>D.J. DIAMOND,<br>Defendant. | CV01-123654<br><br>COMPLAINT; JURY DEMAND |

For its complaint against defendant D.J. Diamond ("Diamond"), plaintiff Paradise Partners ("Paradise") alleges as follows:

1. Paradise is a corporation formed under the laws of the State of Nita and has its principal place of business in Nita City, Nita.

2. Diamond is an individual residing in Los Angeles, California. Diamond is an international recording artist, pop star, and celebrity performing throughout the United States, including the State of Nita.

3. Jurisdiction is proper in this court because this civil action is between citizens of different states and the amount in controversy exceeds $75,000.

4. Venue is proper in this court because the subject contract was entered into and was to be performed in this judicial district, and a substantial part of the events, acts, or omissions giving rise to the claims occurred in this district.

## GENERAL ALLEGATIONS

5. Paradise is a private, not-for-profit organization dedicated to uplifting the lives of underprivileged youth in Nita and surrounding areas, focusing particularly on the diverse and urgent needs of poor and marginalized communities.

6. Each year in June, Paradise hosts a free nature camp near Nita City, Nita, for children aged 8–15 who cannot otherwise afford to attend a camp. The camp hosts multiple sessions of approximately 150 campers and offers sports and recreation (such as softball, basketball, soccer, and creative arts), team-building exercises, and activities promoting nutrition, self-esteem, conflict resolution, and nonviolence. For years, the camp has positively changed the lives of countless children, their families, and their communities.

7. To cover the expenses that Paradise incurs in holding the camp, Paradise and Diamond agreed that Diamond would perform a benefit concert, with Paradise to retain the profits from ticket sales.

8. On or about November 30, YR-2, Paradise and Diamond entered into a contract entitled "Agreement for Concert Performance" ("the agreement"), obligating Diamond to perform a two-hour concert for the public on February 12, YR-1 ("the concert"). Attached as Exhibit A to this complaint is a true and correct copy of the agreement.** Under the agreement, Paradise would pay Diamond the nominal fee of $100, and Paradise would receive the proceeds from the ticket sales, less certain costs and expenses as set forth in the agreement. Paradise and Diamond understood that Paradise would then use those proceeds to fund the camp, and that Paradise was relying on the proceeds for that purpose.

9. In reliance on the agreement and the reasonable expectation that Diamond would perform at the concert, Paradise rented the Nita Amphitheater, an indoor, heated facility, as the concert venue, publicized and marketed the concert, and incurred related costs in an amount to be proved at trial, but not less than $34,500.

10. Tickets to the concert went on sale on January 2, YR-1. The concert sold out within minutes. Gross sale proceeds exceeded $3 million. Paradise would have received a profit of approximately $2.5 million from the concert, which would have allowed Paradise to hold the camp and change hundreds of lives for the better.

11. On February 10, YR-1, just two days before the concert, Diamond, through Diamond's agent and manager Dakota "Doomsday" Dyer ("Doomsday"), texted Paradise that Diamond would not perform at the concert. The text stated: "Sorry, D.J. can't do concert. Cold!! FeelN bad."

12. On or about that same date of February 10, YR-1, Diamond messaged fans on the social media platform FriendMe: "On to LV, my precious Sparklers!!" Rumors ensued on social media, suggesting that Diamond would be making a surprise guest appearance at the Super Bowl halftime show in Las Vegas, which was scheduled for the same date as the concert. Paradise alleges that Diamond was not truly sick when reneging on the obligation to perform at the concert; to the contrary, Diamond reneged out of a selfish and greedy desire to attain the fame of appearing at the Super Bowl, had no right to do so under the agreement, and acted with utter disregard for the harm inflicted on the children and the fans who had paid to see the performance.

13. Despite several attempts to communicate with Diamond and Doomsday, Diamond refused to respond, did not perform at the concert, and breached the agreement.

** The agreement is included as Exhibit 4 in this case file. Assume that it was, in fact, attached to this complaint.

14. Diamond's breach of the agreement forced Paradise to cancel the concert, which it did on February 11, YR-1, and refund all ticket revenue to ticket purchasers. The concert was not held. Losing the concert revenue compelled Paradise to abandon the annual camp, disappointing hundreds of underserved children and their families, causing financial loss to prospective workers at the concert, damaging Paradise's reputation, and forfeiting existing and future donors and donation revenue. In addition, Paradise remained obligated to pay for certain costs incurred in preparing for the concert, in an amount of not less than $34,500.

## FIRST CLAIM FOR RELIEF—BREACH OF CONTRACT

15. Paradise incorporates each and every allegation set forth in paragraphs 1–14 above.
16. Paradise and Diamond entered into the written agreement.
17. Paradise did all, or substantially all, of the significant things that the agreement required it to do or was excused from having to do those things.
18. Diamond breached the agreement by failing to do what the agreement required, including without limitation failing to perform at the concert.
19. Paradise was harmed by Diamond's breach of the agreement.
20. Diamond's breach of contract was a substantial factor in causing Paradise's harm.
21. Therefore, Paradise is entitled to judgment against Diamond as set forth below.

## PRAYER FOR RELIEF

1. For special damages according to proof, including (without limitation) lost profits, future harm, reliance damages, harm to reputation, loss of existing and future donors and donation revenue, and out-of-pocket expenses;
2. For general damages according to proof;
3. For punitive damages according to proof;
4. For costs of suit and attorney fees;
5. For pre-judgment interest and post-judgment interest;
6. For restitution according to proof; and
7. For such other and further relief as the court may deem proper.

## JURY DEMAND

Paradise hereby demands trial by jury.

DATED: March 14, YR-1

______________________

Attorney for Plaintiff

**UNITED STATES DISTRICT COURT**
**NORTHERN DISTRICT OF NITA**

| | |
|---|---|
| PARADISE PARTNERS,<br>Plaintiff,<br><br>v.<br><br>D.J. DIAMOND,<br>Defendant. | CV01-123654<br><br>ANSWER TO COMPLAINT |

D.J. Diamond ("Diamond") answers the complaint of Paradise Partners ("Paradise") as follows:

1. Diamond lacks information to admit or deny the allegations of paragraph 1 of the complaint and therefore denies them.
2. Admit.
3. Admit.
4. Admit.
5. Diamond lacks information to admit or deny the allegations of paragraph 5 of the complaint and therefore denies them.
6. Diamond lacks information to admit or deny the allegations of paragraph 6 of the complaint and therefore denies them.
7. Diamond admits that Diamond agreed to do a benefit concert as set forth in the agreement for contract performance (the agreement). Diamond lacks information to admit or deny the other allegations of paragraph 7 of the complaint and therefore denies them.
8. Diamond admits that the parties entered into the agreement as set forth therein. Except as so admitted, Diamond denies each and every allegation of paragraph 8.
9. Diamond lacks information to admit or deny the allegations of paragraph 9 of the complaint and therefore denies them.
10. Diamond admits that tickets to the concert went on sale on January 2, YR-1, and the concert sold out after tickets went on sale. Except as so admitted, Diamond denies each and every allegation of paragraph 10.
11. Admit.

12. Diamond admits that on February 10, YR-1, Diamond messaged fans on the social media platform known as FriendMe: "On to LV, my precious Sparklers!!" Diamond further admits that rumors on social media suggested that Diamond might appear at the Super Bowl half-time show in Las Vegas, which was scheduled for the same date as the Concert. Except as so admitted, Diamond denies each and every allegation of paragraph 12.

13. Deny.

14. Deny.

15. Diamond incorporates the responses to each and every allegation as set forth in paragraphs 1–14 above.

16. Admit.

17. Deny.

18. Deny.

19. Deny.

20. Deny.

21. Deny.

**AFFIRMATIVE DEFENSES**

1. The complaint does not state a claim for relief.

2. If the contract is not construed as Diamond understands it, the parties were mutually mistaken as to one or more material terms.

3. Paradise failed to mitigate its damages.

4. Diamond's performance was excused due to impossibility or impracticability.

DATED: April 4, YR-1

______________________

Attorney for Defendant

**UNITED STATES DISTRICT COURT**
**NORTHERN DISTRICT OF NITA**

| | |
|---|---|
| PARADISE PARTNERS,<br>Plaintiff,<br><br>v.<br><br>D.J. DIAMOND,<br>Defendant.<br><br>D.J. DIAMOND,<br>Counterclaimant,<br><br>v.<br><br>PARADISE PARTNERS,<br>Counter-Defendant. | CV01-123654<br><br>D.J. DIAMOND'S COUNTERCLAIM AGAINST PARADISE PARTNERS FOR COPYRIGHT INFRINGEMENT |

D.J. Diamond ("Diamond") alleges against Paradise Partners ("Paradise") as follows:

1. Diamond is an individual residing in Los Angeles, California, and is one of the most recognized and influential performing artists in the world.

2. Counter-defendant Paradise is a business entity organized under the laws of the State of Nita with its principal place of business in Nita City, Nita. Its chief executive officer is and was Payton Plaze, who at all relevant times was acting on behalf of Paradise as its agent.

3. Jurisdiction and venue are proper in this court pursuant to Nita Code of Civil Procedure 2424.

## BACKGROUND INFORMATION

4. The Copyright Act (17 N.C.A. §§ 501, et seq.) renders it unlawful to copy, to distribute copies to the public, to display or perform publicly, or to prepare derivative works from any work whose copyright is owned by another, except in limited circumstances not present in this case.

5. Generative artificial intelligence ("GAI") systems, such as the one at issue in this case, use inputs such as text, image, video, audio, and computer code to generate outputs containing new content. The use of GAI systems may result in a violation of copyright laws

in at least two ways. First, inputting a copyrighted work into a GAI system to "train" the system's algorithms or models may infringe the copyright of the inputted work. Second, the output of a GAI system—in the form of a secondary work—infringes the copyright of the original, copyrighted work. As the focus here, a video (output) that Paradise created using a GAI system and without Diamond's permission violates Diamond's copyright.

## GENERAL FACTUAL ALLEGATIONS

6. In early December YR-2, Diamond created a video that included 1) images portraying Diamond speaking and performing, and 2) audio of Diamond's songs and music, as well as Diamond's spoken voice (and graphics) describing, among other things, the date and time of a benefit concert Diamond was going to perform in YR-1 ("original work"). The original work is substantially different from any of the components from which it was assembled. As an original work of authorship fixed in a tangible medium of expression, the original work was and is entitled to copyright protection.

7. At all relevant times, Diamond is and was the exclusive owner of the copyright in the original work under 17 N.C.A. § 106 (as well as the exclusive owner of the copyright in the materials used to create the original work). The copyright office has issued to Diamond a certificate of copyright registration for the original work. As the copyright owner, only Diamond may copy the original work, make derivative works, publicly display or perform copies or derivative works, or distribute copies or derivative works.

8. In mid-December YR-2, Diamond, through Diamond's agent and business manager Dakota "Doomsday" Dyer, provided the original work to Paradise to be used solely to promote the benefit concert Diamond was scheduled to perform in February YR-1. From the date the original work was provided to Paradise, Paradise had access to the original work. In December YR-2, Paradise used the original work to promote the benefit concert.

9. At no point did Diamond authorize Paradise, or anyone on Paradise's behalf, to use the original work, make a copy of the original work, make a derivative work, publicly display a copy of the original work or derivative work, or distribute a copy of the original work or derivative work, except to promote the benefit concert at which Diamond was to perform.

## INFRINGEMENT BY COPYING AND BY CREATING A DERIVATIVE WORK

10. In mid-March YR-1, without Diamond's permission, Paradise uploaded the original work into a GAI application, product, or system with the intent of copying the original work and creating a derivative work that was not for the purpose of promoting the benefit concert.

11. Also in mid-March YR-1, and without Diamond's permission, Paradise used the product, application, or system to create a video that included 1) images portraying Diamond speaking and performing, 2) audio of Diamond's songs and music, as well as what purported to be Diamond's voice making statements that were flattering to Paradise and asking Diamond's fans to donate at least $100 each to Paradise (the "infringing video").

12. The infringing video was not created or used to promote the benefit concert, but to exploit Diamond's name, image, fame, and influence, and to dupe unsuspecting fans into giving money to Paradise. Diamond alleges that Paradise has been successful using the infringing video for this purpose.

13. The infringing video is a copy of the original work in that it is substantially similar (and strikingly similar) to the original work, to which Paradise had access. Among other things, the infringing video includes many of the same images and words as the original work and employs the same style, look, and feel.

14. The ideas, representations, style, and identity of the infringing video was developed based on the ideas, representations, style, and identities of Diamond's copyrighted original work. The infringing video is derivative of Diamond's copyrighted original work.

15. As a copy and a derivative of the original work, the infringing video violates the copyright of the original work.

## INFRINGEMENT OF OTHER COPYRIGHTED SOURCE MATERIAL

16. In addition, in YR-1 and without permission from the copyright holder, Paradise used other images, audio, information, materials, and other data ("source material") besides the original work, including other copyrighted works that were scraped from the internet by Paradise and/or others, to create the infringing video. At no time did Diamond authorize Paradise, or anyone on Paradise's behalf, to make a copy of any other work for which Diamond owns the copyright, or to make a derivative work, publicly display a copy or derivative work, or distribute a copy or derivative work. The infringing video therefore violates the copyrights of the source material, as well as the copyright of the original work.

## INFRINGEMENT BY DISTRIBUTING, DISPLAYING, PERFORMING

17. On or about March 24, YR-1, and without permission from Diamond for use of the original work or any copyright holder of any other source material, Paradise distributed and displayed the infringing video, including portions of the original work, by releasing it to the public through its website, social media platforms, and other media channels.

18. Paradise has refused to pay Diamond any amount for its infringing uses of the original work.

19. As a proximate result of Paradise's conduct, Diamond has suffered, and will continue to suffer, damages in an amount to be proved at trial.

20. Paradise prospered by its violation of Diamond's copyright on the original work, and Paradise must disgorge to Diamond all profits of Paradise that are attributable to the infringement (to the extent not awarded as actual damages).

21. Diamond alleges that Paradise used the copyrighted original work of Diamond, as well as the copyrighted works of others, with the result of exposing those works to the public and contributing to the training of various GAI systems, thereby contributing to additional violations of the copyright act perpetrated by others. Diamond intends to seek leave to amend this complaint to allege such additional and further acts of copyright infringements and resulting damages, which are in addition to the damages presently alleged.

22. By virtue of Paradise's alleged acts, Diamond is entitled to statutory damages (17 N.C.A. §§ 501, et seq.). In addition, Paradise's infringement of copyright was knowing, willful, and intentional, and Paradise is therefore liable to Diamond for statutory damages for willful infringement.

23. Diamond has suffered, or is likely to suffer, an irreparable injury in the absence of an injunction. Remedies at law are inadequate to compensate Diamond for this injury. An equitable remedy is required in light of the balance of the hardships to the parties. The public interest will not be disserved by the issuance of temporary and permanent injunctions.

## PRAYER FOR RELIEF

1. Actual damages, including without limitation

    a. the fair market value of a license to use the original work as Paradise has used it, and

    b. lost profits, both incurred and in the future, suffered by Diamond as a result of the infringement.

2. Disgorgement of Paradise's profits from its infringement;

3. Statutory damages, including statutory damages for willful infringement;

4. Reasonable attorney fees pursuant to 17 N.C.A. § 505;

5. Costs of this suit;

6. A temporary and permanent injunction restraining Paradise from using the infringing video in any way that violates Diamond's copyright; and

7. Such other and further relief as the court may deem proper.

DATED: April 4, YR-1

____________________________

Attorney for Counterclaimant

**UNITED STATES DISTRICT COURT**
**NORTHERN DISTRICT OF NITA**

| | |
|---|---|
| PARADISE PARTNERS,<br>Plaintiff,<br><br>v.<br><br>D.J. DIAMOND,<br>Defendant.<br><br>D.J. DIAMOND,<br>Counterclaimant<br><br>v.<br><br>PARADISE PARTNERS,<br>Counter-Defendant. | CV01-123654<br><br>PARADISE PARTNERS' ANSWER TO DIAMOND'S COUNTERCLAIM FOR COPYRIGHT INFRINGEMENT |

Pursuant to Nita Code of Civil Procedure section 2221, Paradise Partners ("Paradise") denies each and every allegation of the counterclaim of D.J. Diamond ("Diamond").

## AFFIRMATIVE DEFENSES

1. The counterclaim fails to state a claim for relief.
2. The alleged infringement purportedly occurred before a certificate of copyright registration was issued, and no certificate of copyright registration was issued within three months of the publication of the work. Diamond is therefore not entitled to statutory damages or attorney fees.
3. Paradise had an express license to use the copyrighted work in the manner alleged.
4. Paradise had an implied license to use the copyrighted work in the manner alleged.
5. Paradise's use of the copyrighted work, if any, is protected under the fair use doctrine.
6. Under the laches doctrine, Paradise cannot be held liable due to the passage of time.
7. Diamond is estopped from recovering on the alleged claims.
8. Diamond has waived the right to recover on the alleged claims.

9. Diamond is not entitled to recover due to Diamond's unclean hands.

10. Diamond is not entitled to recover due to Diamond's copyright misuse.

DATED: May 2, YR-1

____________________________

Attorney for Counter-Defendant
Paradise Partners

# Depositions

# Deposition of Payton Plaze

My name is Payton Plaze. I am 32 years old. I've been married to my spouse, Price Plaze, for ten years. We have two adopted children, aged two and four. We live in Verdugo Heights, a suburb of Nita City.

I'm a product of my background. I was removed from my biological parents by child welfare workers when I was around three years old, I'm told, and raised in a series of foster homes. I have no fond memories of my first two foster families—I was scared and lonely, and it was really rough. In my third foster home, however, I hit the jackpot. My foster parents, whom I still call Mom and Dad, took me in when I was nine and eventually adopted me. They taught me self-esteem and the value of hard work, perseverance, faith, and education. They also instilled in me a compassion for others.

It all paid off. Thanks to my foster parents, I became the valedictorian of Nita City High School and captain of my swim team. After graduating high school in YR-14, I received a scholarship to Stanford University. I graduated from Stanford in YR-10 with honors and a BS in computer science. My focus was on software programming.

About a month after graduating from Stanford, I took a job as a programmer at the tech company Hooray! Not long after that, the concept of artificial intelligence (AI) gained wider interest and I became a member of Hooray!'s machine learning team, designing and improving on company AI. Still, I felt like a mere cog in the Hooray! machine and wasn't satisfied.

In YR-7, two coworkers and I saw the chance to impact the world more directly. We quit Hooray! to start our own company, Live Forever, which was going to focus on using AI to provide personalized health programs for individuals. Essentially, we created algorithms that synthesize an individual's DNA, family history, and health history to provide guidance on that person's ideal diet, exercise, mindfulness, and spirituality for a long and full life.

Because Live Forever was a start-up, my compensation was low but I received stock options that vested and became exercisable in YR-4. I exercised the options that same year, and within a few months Live Forever went public. Around that time, however, I became disenchanted with Live Forever as it veered from our original mission—improving people's lives—toward using AI to clone individuals and replace them. In YR-4, I resigned from Live Forever, sold almost all my stock, and became a multi-millionaire overnight.

Later in YR-4, I founded Paradise Partners and became its executive director, which I still am today. Paradise is a private 501(c)(3) organization dedicated to uplifting the lives of underprivileged youth. It reflects both my zeal for scientific and spiritual means of prolonging a joyful life and my deep desire to meet the needs of youth who, like me, could easily go astray without the intervention of a few caring adults. I'm passionate about transforming the lives of underprivileged children. When asked why I left tech and the big bucks, I just say, "It's all for the children."

Paradise is located in Nita City. It serves its community year-round, offering academic counseling and mentoring services, nutritional education, a food bank, a 24-hour indoor basketball court, and after-school programs including dance instruction, arts and crafts, and even a coding class for kids that I teach myself. Paradise has fifteen to twenty employees depending on the season, as well as quite a few volunteers. As executive director, I am the face of the company, reporting to our board of directors and overseeing day-to-day operations and our strategic vision. Under me are our primary leadership positions—director of operations, director of finance, director of fundraising, director of programming, and director of communications. Each of the directors supervises just a couple of employees—we run a lean ship. We don't have in-house counsel, but we have a relationship with two law firms in Nita City.

Pat Paw is my assistant director of fundraising. I hired Pat because Pat was the best candidate for the job. Well, Pat was the only candidate, at least the only candidate my spouse, Price, told me to hire. Price knows Pat's mother from yoga class. When I hired Pat in February YR-2, we didn't have much of a need for an assistant director of fundraising—and that was good because Pat didn't have the best employment history. As I recall, Pat had bounced from one job to another, and although I'm used to that in tech, it seemed Pat wasn't doing well at work and ran into a lot of bad luck. I wasn't too concerned because we already had a great director of fundraising, Happy Hunter, who could easily do the fundraising work. Sadly, though, Hunter vanished on April 1, YR-2, no one knows where. Since then, Pat has been the de facto fundraising director, although I haven't promoted Pat to Hunter's position.

In addition to the year-round activities I've already described, Paradise's main event each year is hosting a free nature camp for hundreds of children who could not otherwise afford to attend a camp. It's held in June for children aged 8–15, and foster children have priority enrollment. The camp includes sports and recreational activities, team-building exercises, and programs on nutrition, self-esteem, conflict resolution, and paths to non-violence and freedom from chemical dependence. We hold it at a campsite shared with other nonprofits in Lost Valley, a few miles outside Nita City. The camp has four one-week sessions; campers can sign up for one week or two. Each session has up to 150 campers. We call it, "Camp 2 Belong."

Running the camp is expensive. We rent the campsite and pay for staff, food, insurance, and more, totaling about $500,000 annually.

Exhibit 21 appears to be a fair and accurate depiction of our revenue and expenses, including fundraising numbers, over the years. Yes, I initially donated $3,000,000 of my personal funds to Paradise Partners to hire staff, build out our space, and pay for the camp at least for the first year. Obviously, $3,000,000 wasn't enough to do the build-out and keep all the programming running indefinitely. That's why I hired fundraisers to make sure that we had a steady income stream, through both donations and grants. In YR-2, we knew my initial $3,000,000 capital investment would be depleted and we wouldn't have enough money to fund the camp in YR-1.

In November YR-2, Pat and I were discussing how we could raise enough funds to put on the YR-1 camp. We considered holding another gala, which would bring in some funds but not enough—the expenses for an event like that are sky high, but if you don't throw a really upscale party then people won't attend. Pat said we could start a FundMeNow page and solicit donations, which was unrealistic, but it got me thinking that we could raise a lot more money if we had celebrities touting what we do and encouraging their fans to donate. Then one of us came up with the idea of having a benefit concert, where we'd get a celebrity to do a concert and we'd receive the profits. Pat literally jumped up and shrieked, "I'm good friends with D.J. Diamond!" the famous pop singer. I think they even dated for a while. So, I asked Pat to contact Diamond about it.

Pat contacted Diamond, and Diamond agreed to do the concert. When Pat told me the good news in late November YR-2, it was hard to believe. Pat had experience negotiating contracts from a previous accounting job, so I asked Pat to pursue the contract with Diamond's business manager but to keep me informed and to run everything past our lawyers. Our general idea was that we'd want the concert to be in February YR-1, because the deadline for canceling a reservation with the camp facility was in March.

I wasn't involved in the contract negotiations. But I do recognize the concert contract in Exhibit 4 because Pat sent it to me after it was signed in December YR-2. I wish Pat had sent it to me before signing it, but that's water under the bridge. Yes, Pat was authorized to sign the contract on Paradise's behalf. As I understood it, the contract required Diamond to perform a two-hour set for $100, and all net proceeds from ticket sales would go to Paradise. Paradise was going to use those proceeds to fund the camp. The benefit concert was set for February 12, YR-1.

None of us at Paradise knew anything about putting on concerts. We turned to an outfit called Concerts-R-Us, who gave us a package deal. From December YR-2 to February YR-1, Concerts-R-Us secured the concert venue (the Nita City Amphitheater), arranged for food vendors, staffing, and security; confirmed that all the equipment Diamond needed would be there; marketed the concert; and sold concert tickets. As I understand it, a concert promoter usually gets the artist and the venue (and related vendors and workers) and does the marketing, sells the tickets, collects the money, and then distributes the funds to the artists etc. Here, we already had the artist, but Concerts-R-Us was willing to do the rest. Exhibit 5 is the contract with Concerts-R-Us. I know nothing else about what Concerts-R-Us did or how they did it.

Pat told me that the concert sold out within minutes after tickets went on sale on January 2, YR-1. The gross proceeds from the ticket sales were well over $3 million, and we were slated to get about $2 million net out of it. We were ecstatic!

But our joy turned to despair. On February 10, YR-1, just two days before the concert, Pat came to my office wide-eyed, saying that Diamond was sick and couldn't perform the concert. Pat showed me a text from Diamond's business manager, Dakota "Doomsday" Dyer. Yes, Exhibit 6 is a copy of that text. It states: "Sorry, Diamond can't do concert. FeelN bad." Pat said neither Diamond nor Doomsday returned Pat's calls and texts. I told Pat to keep trying to reach them, while I'd figure out what to do.

Later that night, I saw that Diamond messaged fans on FriendMe: "On to LV, my precious Sparklers!!" Exhibit 8 is a copy of the message. I also saw some buzz on social media that Diamond was making a surprise appearance at the Super Bowl half-time show in Las Vegas, which was scheduled for the day of the benefit concert. I suspected that Diamond was not really sick but simply reneged on the benefit concert to get the fame of appearing at the Super Bowl.

Diamond's backing out was obviously crushing news for us, for ticketholders, for the concert workers, for the children planning to attend the camp and their families, and for all the people who were going to be camp counselors, teachers, cooks, and staff. Thousands of people had already purchased tickets, and now there was no way we could do the concert. Not only did Diamond hurt us, Diamond hurt a bunch of "precious Sparklers."

On February 10, YR-1, I emailed Doomsday. I implored Doomsday to convince Diamond to fulfill the terms of the contract. Exhibit 9 is copy of my email. I never heard back.

On February 11, YR-1, the day before the concert date, we issued an announcement on our website and social media that the concert was canceled due to Diamond's unavailability and circumstances beyond our control. Exhibit 11 is a copy of the announcement. We refunded all the ticket proceeds through Concerts-R-Us. We were still out the costs of securing the venue and other expenses incurred to Concerts-R-Us, amounting to something like $34,500, which we paid. We have no funds for the camp.

On February 12, YR-1 (the day that had been set for the concert), I wrote and sent a letter to Doomsday, expressing my disappointment in Diamond's cancellation and my suspicion that Diamond was not truly sick and had wrongfully reneged on the concert contract. Exhibit 12 is my letter. No, there were no earlier drafts. Yes, I watched the Super Bowl halftime show and noticed that Diamond did not perform. Nevertheless, I think Diamond faked the illness—Diamond did travel to Las Vegas, so couldn't have been very sick, if at all.

A few days later, I received a really obnoxious and insulting letter from Doomsday telling me basically that Diamond did not breach the contract. Exhibit 14 is a copy of the letter. Doomsday made some ridiculous excuse that the contract allowed Diamond to back out if it was to Diamond's financial advantage. That doesn't make any sense. Nearly any opportunity Diamond got would have been to Diamond's financial advantage, because Diamond was only going to receive $100 for performing at the benefit concert. Why would we pay tens of thousands of dollars to put on a benefit concert that Diamond could back out of at the last minute? Besides, I doubt Diamond was going to be paid anything for the Super Bowl appearance.

We canceled the campsite reservation in March, YR-2. I was heartbroken, but we just didn't have the money due to Diamond's breach.

On behalf of Paradise, I authorized our lawyers to sue Diamond for what we lost when Diamond refused to perform, because the cancellation was not due to Diamond's "mental or physical health, security, or well-being" as required by the cancellation provision of the concert contract.

In a press release, I vowed to use all amounts recovered from the lawsuit to fund the camp and other Paradise projects for underprivileged youth. Exhibit 15 is the press release. And yes, the press release contains a typo. The word "pony" should have been "penny." I wish Pat had been more careful proofreading—you can't imagine how many people have sent me plastic ponies and pony jokes.

After we filed the lawsuit, I still wanted to generate income to cover our payment to Concerts-R-Us and to fund a future camp or cover operating expenses. I remembered that Doomsday had provided video footage of Diamond in December YR-2—including footage of Diamond saying how great Paradise is. Exhibit 19 is a copy of the video, along with a transcription of the text. Pat forwarded the footage to Concerts-R-Us before tickets went on sale, and they used it for marketing. I thought it would be fair for us to create a new video in which Diamond said the same things about Paradise but in the context of soliciting monetary contributions rather than ticket sales.

In March YR-1, I uploaded various material to an app called DeepestPhakes Live 3.0 to create the new video. Specifically, I uploaded the footage received from Doomsday and other footage that I had downloaded from the internet as my source data, along with another organization's promo spot as my target video. I told the app what I wanted Diamond to say. To make the switch from Diamond's original words to the new words seem realistic, I uploaded a separate vocal track that I created from another app, which applied Diamond's voice to the words. Then I clicked "Go" and let the app do its thing. The initial output was okay, but I had to train the app a bit with more definite instructions, which modified the output until I got what I thought was pretty cool and realistic. I just followed the prompts on the app. The whole thing took me about an hour.

The new video is very different from the footage Doomsday sent to me. It's basically a deepfake video of Diamond praising Paradise and urging all of Diamond's fans to send Paradise at least $100 or as much as they can. Exhibit 20 is a copy of the video that I created as well as the transcription of the text. At my direction, our IT people uploaded the new video to our website and social media platforms, such as our page on FriendMe, on March 24, YR-1.

No, I wasn't mad or trying to hurt Diamond when I created the video. It was all for the children. Well, ok, since you've continued to press me on it, I admit I was a bit ticked off at Doomsday and Diamond initially, but I truly thought it would be fair to use Diamond's image to get what we should have gotten if Diamond hadn't flaked. That's what you call "fair use," right? And I actually put Diamond in a very favorable light, so it seemed like a win-win to me. After all, Diamond is the one who made the original video footage worthless by cancelling the concert, and neither Diamond nor Doomsday ever said I couldn't use the video footage they gave me. I never would have made the video if I thought it was illegal or wrong.

Less than an hour after uploading the new video, we started receiving donations, which eventually totaled $518,200. We were happy to have the money, but this was way less than the profit we would have obtained from the concert. It was also too late to reserve the campsite.

Sure, I've seen the articles and blog posts about the concert, but Paradise barely gets mentioned. It's all about Diamond. How are we supposed to use that to earn money? "D.J. Diamond scammed us, so give us money"? We'd be back in this office with a defamation lawsuit in no time.

How do I feel about Pat now? About the same. Pat is well-meaning and tenderhearted and just needs some guidance. How do I feel about Diamond and Doomsday? Well, they were wrong, but I forgive them. That's what we're supposed to do, right?

# Deposition of Pat Paw

My name is Pat Paw. I'm 24 years old. I grew up in Nita City, graduated from Nita City High School in YR-6, and still live in Nita City with my mom.

I didn't want to go to college, so after high school I started working at the grocery store chain, Trapper John's. I stocked shelves and was eventually promoted to checker, but I was let go in YR-4. I just couldn't get my cash drawer to balance. From YR-4 to YR-2, I worked odd jobs—mowing lawns, driving for an online food delivery service, and doing filing and other clerical tasks at an accounting office. I also walked dogs as a side gig for a few weeks, until one of the dogs escaped. Fortunately, the dog's owner calmed down after finding her pooch on her porch.

In February of YR-2, Payton Plaze hired me to be assistant director of fundraising at Paradise Partners. My mom told me about the job, and I think Payton hired me as a favor to her. My job interview was brief; I don't really remember it.

When I started working at Paradise, I just shadowed the director of fundraising, Happy Hunter. But Hunter disappeared on April Fool's Day, YR-2. No one has seen Hunter since. I took over the director of fundraising duties, although my title is still assistant director of fundraising. Payton hasn't hired anyone to replace Hunter. No, I haven't received any formal training—just what Hunter showed me on the job and what I can figure out from Hunter's files.

My duties as assistant director of fundraising consist of the following: creating an annual fundraising plan that sets goals and identifies sources of income; corresponding with donors; and organizing events to honor existing donors, attract new ones, and raise funds. It's gone great!

Well, sure, there have been a couple of hiccups along the way. One of last year's fundraisers was a silent auction, and I didn't catch an error in the address on our invitation—11911 Worthington Avenue instead of 19111 Worthington Avenue—so only two people showed up. We actually lost money after subtracting for catering costs and such. And for last year's gala for loyal donors, I decided to have a petting zoo for the kids. It was such a great idea, but only a llama, a pig, and six chickens were delivered. The llama kept spitting at the children, the pig trampled the chickens' pen, and the chickens escaped and started running all around the guests in the dining room. Despite all the shrieks and screaming, I think everyone had a good time watching me chase down those chickens. But when I told Payton it was time to plan the YR-1 gala, the response I got was lukewarm. Payton wanted to find a new direction for fundraising.

Working at Paradise is pretty cool. It's a great organization that helps underprivileged kids. It's located in Nita City. We do things like helping kids with homework and giving nutritional and career advice. We keep our indoor basketball court open to members 24 hours, and we have after-school programs with classes and arts and crafts. Payton is the executive director, and Paradise employs a dozen or so people besides me, plus a lot of volunteers. We have departments for operations, finance, fundraising, programs, and communications. Payton's a good person to work for and deeply believes in Paradise. You always hear Payton saying, "It's all for the children."

Paradise's main event of the year is a free nature camp for children, aged 8–15, who can't otherwise afford to attend a camp. We hold it every June at a campsite a few miles outside Nita City in Lost Valley. There are four one-week sessions, and campers can sign up for one or two sessions. Each session, we host approximately 150 campers. The campers are divided into twelve cabins of about twelve, sometimes thirteen kids; each cabin has an adult leader, a leader in training, and a name like Team One Owls, Team Two Tigers, etc. The camp includes sports and recreation, like basketball, soccer, softball, and arts. I'm hoping to add archery. The camp also offers team-building exercises and activities promoting nutrition, self-esteem, conflict resolution, and non-violence. I know the camp has been a life changer for a lot of the kids. For some, it's the first time they've been out of the city. For many, it's the first time they've had people care about them and love on them.

In the last months of YR-2, we realized that Paradise couldn't afford to do the camp in June YR-1 because donations have been down ever since, well, the "hide and seek incident." I had nothing to do with that, by the way. In YR-2, one of the campers hid and we never found him. The cops located him a few days later—in some bar in St. Louis, I think—so it all worked out.

How did the idea for the benefit concert come up? Well, one day, sometime in November YR-2, Payton was talking with a bunch of us employees in the break room about how we might raise funds for the YR-1 camp. Someone said we should have a benefit concert. So, I let everyone know I was best friends with D.J. Diamond, and I could probably convince D.J. to do the concert. Everyone started freaking out because D.J. is so famous. It was cool—everybody was in awe of me knowing D.J. People asked for backstage passes, and I said sure, I could arrange them. Yeah, I felt really important. I was the hero, saving the camp and getting Nita City an amazing concert.

In hindsight, it might have been an overstatement to say that D.J. and I were best friends. I mean, D.J. was very nice to me in grade school—waving hello and sometimes even letting me sit at the same table at lunch. During middle school and high school, D.J. was away a lot but I followed D.J.'s career very closely. Yes, I'm a "Sparkler"—the nickname for D.J.'s fans. In fact, I'm the unofficial president of D.J.'s fan club and I have all D.J.'s music on my phone. I still have three posters of D.J. in my bedroom, along with a few photos we took in grade school and almost all the "merch" (T-shirts, water bottles, etc.) from D.J.'s website.

The whole Diamond family moved to LA after high school graduation, but I still had D.J.'s cell number even though we hadn't talked for a while. I was kind of shy about calling, but Payton and everybody else kept asking if I'd heard anything, so I got brave and texted D.J. on November 28, YR-2. Exhibit 1 is that text and D.J.'s response from that same day.

D.J. asked when and where the concert would be. I suggested February because of deadlines for reserving the camp facility in March. And I said it would be in Nita City because Payton and I had figured that made sense, since Paradise is located here and it's where D.J. grew up.

Surprisingly, D.J. texted back right away, excited to do the concert—"wouldn't miss it for the world"—and gave me the number for Dakota "Doomsday" Dyer, to do the paperwork. Doomsday is D.J.'s business manager.

I immediately told Payton that D.J. would perform and we had to contact the business manager to work out the contract. I might have mentioned to Payton that I negotiated contracts at my earlier accounting job. Payton said something like, "what are you waiting for," and so I called Doomsday. Doomsday didn't answer, so I left a voicemail message. I don't remember what I said in my message.

It might have been an exaggeration to say I negotiated contracts at the accounting office. I did place contracts into file folders there, but I'd never actually negotiated a contract, except some oral contracts when I walked people's dogs. But as it turns out, there wasn't any negotiating with Doomsday anyway, so no harm no foul, right?

While I was waiting for Doomsday to call me back, I realized I didn't know anything about big-time concert promotions, so I googled and found the local office of a business called Concerts-R-Us and called them. Concerts-R-Us specializes in concert promotion. I talked to this nice guy, Rock, who explained they would just need to see the contract and work with D.J.'s manager on some details. Rock told me it was difficult to put together a big concert in the amount of time we had, but because Diamond was already signed and they had connections with the 15,000-seat Nita City Amphitheater and a bunch of vendors, they were able to do it. He started to tell me the financial stuff but I just asked him to put it in a letter and he said okay. Our call was on November 29, YR-2.

Anyway, Doomsday called me back, or maybe I called Doomsday again, and we spoke on November 29 or 30, YR-2, for about five minutes. Doomsday told me the concert would have to be on February 12, YR-1, which was fine with us since the camp wasn't until June. Doomsday said D.J. would do a two-hour set for a nominal fee of $100, and Paradise would get the ticket proceeds to fund the camp. I told Doomsday that Concerts-R-Us would handle the venue, marketing, and ticket sales, and I gave Doomsday Rock's contact information. I did take some notes of my conversation with Doomsday. Exhibit 3 is my notes—please excuse the doodles. It's my regular procedure to take notes of important business conversations and keep them in a file.

Yes, my notes mention "promo vid," which refers to a promotional video. Because of the silent auction fiasco, I wanted to make sure all the advertising was right, so I started to tell Doomsday that we needed something to promote the concert. Doomsday cut me off and promised to send over some video footage of D.J. that we could use however we like. I remember this distinctly, because I thought wow, I could so use that footage on a Sparkler webpage I was wanting to build. I later received it electronically and forwarded a copy to Concerts-R-Us. No, I don't remember anything else about my conversation with Doomsday. Okay, since you've pressed me on this, my diary might have something more about it, but I don't show my diary to anyone.

Doomsday sent me the concert contract through DocExecute on November 30, YR-2. I looked the contract over, but I didn't pay much attention because I'm not good with legal stuff. Besides, Doomsday didn't say I could make any changes. So, I made sure that we'd be paying D.J. $100 for a two-hour set on February 12, signed and returned the contract using DocExecute, and informed Payton. No, I didn't run the contract past any lawyers—like I said, we don't have lawyers at Paradise. Yes, I was authorized to sign on Paradise's behalf, because Payton assigned me to get the contract. Exhibit 4, with the heading "Agreement for Concert Performance," is a copy of the contract.

Beginning in December YR-2 or so, Concerts-R-Us got us the Nita City Amphitheater, arranged for food vendors, staffing, and security, confirmed that all the equipment Diamond needed would be there, marketed the concert, and sold concert tickets. Exhibit 5 is a copy of our agreement with Concerts-R-Us. Their letter gave me some insights into the business of music concerts, and I don't have any reason to doubt that Concerts-R-Us did everything they said they would. Concerts-R-Us figured we'd probably get over $2 million from the concert, so we were super-hyped.

Tickets went on sale on January 2, YR-2, and the concert sold out within minutes! We were so excited. We knew that we would be able to hold the camp, which costs about $500,000 to put on, and change hundreds of lives.

Yes, I know the concert contract contained a cancellation provision. I see that it stated, "Performer further reserves the right to cancel performer's performance obligations under the agreement for any reason related to performer's mental or physical health, security, or well-being, and in such case shall waive the performance fee but may retain any deposit at performer's sole discretion." I have a vague memory of reading this around the time I signed the contract. I didn't think too much about it, because I believed Diamond was too good of a person to cancel. The provision refers to a deposit, but I don't think we paid one.

No, I don't recall Doomsday ever telling me that Diamond would perform "unless Diamond got a better offer," although I do remember that we laughed about something when we spoke on the phone that day. I also remember telling Doomsday that I would lose my job if Diamond didn't perform because Paradise was investing a lot of money into the concert.

Now that I focus on it, the phrase "well-being" in the cancellation provision obviously refers to how well D.J. feels, to protect against something unexpected happening that would affect D.J.'s health and make it impossible to do the concert. There's no way it could mean D.J.'s financial gain. D.J. told me that they wouldn't miss the concert for the world, and I had told Doomsday that we were putting a lot of money into the concert. Under the circumstances, it wouldn't make any sense to agree to a contract for a free concert that D.J. could get out of just because D.J. could make money doing something else. I never agreed to that, and I never would have signed the contract if that is what Doomsday or D.J. intended.

Just two days before the concert, Doomsday texted me that D.J. was not going to do the concert because D.J. had a cold and wasn't feeling well. I was, like, what? I mean, I was shocked. I texted Doomsday back, but I don't remember what I said. Oh, now that you've shown me my text, I recall that I responded with "What? Oh no! Are you kidding me?" and a shocked face emoji. Exhibit 6 is a copy of Doomsday's text and my response. I received no reply from Doomsday.

Right after texting Doomsday, I texted D.J. I was frantic, hyperventilating even. As shown in Exhibit 7, I actually sent a bunch of texts, pleading with D.J. to do the concert. (I'm not sure why I said I wouldn't have a job; no, Payton didn't tell me that.) I didn't receive any response to my texts—yeah, I got ghosted. I also called Doomsday but there was no answer, and I don't remember what voicemail message I left.

Later that day, Diamond sent a message to fans saying: "On to LV, my precious Sparklers!!" Exhibit 8 is a copy of the message. I showed Payton both Doomsday's text and Diamond's message. (Yes, I know it was around 6pm, but we were still both in the office.) Notifications started firing off on our phones, and we saw social media rumors that Diamond would be making a surprise guest appearance at the Super Bowl halftime show in Las Vegas, the very day of the benefit concert. We started thinking that Diamond was not truly sick, but instead reneged on our concert to get the fame of appearing at the Super Bowl.

I don't remember Exhibit 9. Yes, I see that it's an email from Payton to Doomsday and I'm cc'd on it, but I just don't remember it. I don't recall ever seeing a response either.

Without D.J., Paradise had to cancel the concert and refund all the ticket money. We had no choice. There was no way to get another act, and people bought tickets to see Diamond, not anyone else. Besides, we could never get hold of D.J. or Doomsday to discuss a possible work-around—such as postponing the concert rather than cancelling—and to tell you the truth, I don't think Payton would ever work with Diamond or Doomsday again.

Our cancellation announcement went out on February 11, YR-1. Exhibit 11 is a copy of the announcement.

Not only were we not going to get the funds we'd need to put on the camp, we were out the costs of securing the concert venue. I called Rock at Concerts-R-Us about the cancellation on February 11, YR-1. Shortly after that, I got a letter from Rock saying we owed around $34,500 for reserving the Nita City Amphitheater and the costs for what they did. At my request, they also ran the numbers and told me that, based on the ticket sales and revenue, Paradise would have received over $2.5 million if the concert went forward. I mean, I can't get over it: instead of raising $2.5 million, seeing Diamond, and helping the kids, we owe $34K and have no money to help the kids with camp. What a punch to the gut. Rock's letter is Exhibit 13.

Yes, I do seem to recall that Payton sent a letter to Doomsday, and Doomsday sent one back. The letters are in Exhibits 12 and 14. I don't think it led to anything—certainly the problem didn't get resolved. Eventually, Paradise filed a lawsuit against D.J. for breaching the contract. I think Payton took a lot of heat from donors about the whole fiasco.

We ended up without funds for the camp or any way to raise them. We weren't going to try another benefit concert, and we had no one to ask to do one anyway. To avoid forfeiting our deposit at the campsite, we canceled our reservation in March YR-1 and didn't hold the camp (sign-ups are usually in May), disappointing hundreds of children and infuriating our donors. In fact, as time went on, our usual donation streams dried up as Payton tried to reassure everyone that we would be back in action and running the camp the next year. It took some time for people to start donating to us again. And I gotta say, our donation levels have never recovered. I don't know if we're ever going to be able to put on a camp again.

Exhibit 21 is a fair and accurate depiction of how much we were receiving in donations and grants each year from YR-4 and YR-1. An estimate for YR-0 is included too. This year, we're hoping to get back to around $750,000 in donations again and we have that much pledged, plus some grant money. What the Exhibit 21 chart leaves out is that, when founding Paradise Partners, Payton put $3,000,000 into the account to get things going.

Payton was upset about what D.J. and Doomsday did, as anyone would be. (Personally, I blame Doomsday—D.J. must be under Doomsday's spell or something.) So, Payton decided to get back some of the money we should have made from the concert by creating a video of D.J. encouraging people to donate to Paradise. This was sometime in March YR-1, and it was pretty cool. I wasn't present when Payton made it, but Payton later told me that it involved taking the footage we got from Doomsday to market the concert, uploading it to some app along with other things from the internet about D.J., and instructing the app to create the video. Payton may have used another app to make what Payton was saying on the video sound like D.J.'s voice. It's called "generation AI," I think. Our marketing people put it out there, and right away donations started to hit our website. We received half a million dollars over the next two weeks, which we wouldn't have received without the video. But that was far less than the profit Paradise would have made from the concert. Anyway, with the money that came in, we covered what we owed Concerts-R-Us and the rest went into our operating account. It was too late to put on the camp for YR-1.

Have we taken out any ads online? No; we don't have the money for that! We're a nonprofit, and Payton's had to put in more money just to keep the lights on.

Despite all that happened, I still have a good relationship with Payton. I think Payton understands that D.J.'s reneging on the concert wasn't my fault. I have to say that my view of D.J. has changed a little, though. I always thought D.J. had a beautiful voice, a beautiful face, and a beautiful heart. One of those is clearly not true, and it makes me sad.

[ADDITIONAL TESTIMONY IF COUNTERCLAIM HAS BEEN FILED:]

After Payton's video was released, Doomsday sued us back, saying we didn't have permission to do the video. We clearly had permission. Doomsday is the one who gave us the video, and if we showed that one, D.J. would look horrible advertising a concert and then not doing it. Payton actually did D.J. a favor by adding words and photos and making a video that showed D.J. cared about the children and was generously supporting us. The video was no skin off D.J.'s back—D.J. ended up smelling like a rose, as usual.

# Deposition of D.J. Diamond

My name is D. J. Diamond, and I am 24 years old. It was clear from the time I was born that I was destined to become famous, so when I was three years old my family moved from Cleveland, Ohio, to Nita City, just outside Manhattan. My parents are both in finance, so moving so close to New York made sense for their careers, too.

From before the time that I could walk, I was on screen. I was an unusually attractive baby and I started out in commercials. As I got older, my parents enrolled me in acting and singing classes where I developed my natural talent. I started getting roles on kids' shows like *Look at Me* and *Junior High Dance Party*. In my freshman year of high school, the stars aligned and I was cast as the main character in *Diamond's Devotion*, where I played a famous singer. My career really took off because of *Diamond's Devotion*. In addition to being on the show, I got a percentage of the sales of *Diamond's Devotion* albums and merchandise like T-shirts and posters.

While in high school, I also established my own successful lifestyle brand called Sparkles. I have a Sparkles store online and a brick-and-mortar Sparkles store in Los Angeles. I sell everything from T-shirts and baseball caps to serenity beads. My fans—I call them Sparklers—have always responded well to me because I am so down to earth and relatable. I am real and genuine, and they can see themselves in me. I think that explains why the store was immediately popular, and I was a multi-millionaire before I was 18 years old.

After four years of top-rated episodes on *Diamond's Devotion*, I felt that the universe was calling me to do even more for the world. So, in YR-6 I moved to Los Angeles, where I am very involved in my wellness line, and I also began doing lots of concerts both in the United States and internationally.

Much of YR-2 was spent on my "Diamonds are Forever" tour, involving dozens of cities and dozens of performances over several months. When on tour, I travel in a private jet with my manager and a few others, and we have lots of trucks and planes transporting all the sets and equipment from city to city. I don't know exactly how much I make from the tour and merchandise—my manager takes care of all that—but it's in the millions. The point is that I travel the globe spreading love and positive energy. There's so much suffering and pain out there, and my concerts make people happy. Everything I do to nurture healing brings me joy.

But it's not always easy. Moving around so much means that every new hotel I check into gets instructions for what I like. Yes, I have a private jet and I stay at five-star hotels, so you might think that everything would go smoothly. But it definitely doesn't.

For example, my team is constantly having to remind the hotels where we stay that I'm pescatarian, and that I need my suite stocked with white towels that are only made from ethically-sourced Egyptian cotton because my skin is sensitive. You won't believe it, but just last week my hotel put snacks in my room that included M&M's—and no one had removed the blue ones! I was, like, totally shocked. I've told everyone a thousand times that I cannot eat blue

M&Ms—blue dye is poison. My body is a temple, and I take seriously what I put into it. I told my team never to book that hotel again.

It's worth all the hardship, though, because as someone who believes in karma, it's the right thing for me to use my talents to serve others. That is why I create music and sing, that is why I put so much work into each of my performances, and that is why I just launched my new line of Centered Spirit Aromatherapy Oils.

My amazing manager is Dakota Dyer. I call Dakota "Doomsday" because, well, now I can't remember why. I've known Doomsday for years, and there's complete trust between us. Doomsday always has my back. OMG no, nothing romantic—Doomsday is, like, super old.

Doomsday is always reminding me that, in addition to all the incredible work I'm already doing, it's important for me to be seen doing charity events. So, when I got a text from Pat Paw asking me to do a fundraiser for Paradise Partners, of course I said yes. Exhibit 1 is a copy of our texts.

I googled Paradise Partners, and its website says they are all about doing sports and arts and crafts and tutoring for underprivileged kids, and they run some kind of summer camp that none of the kids can afford. Even though I'm a celebrity, I'm the kind of person who likes to give to others without asking for anything in return. Also, Pat and I knew each other in grade school in Nita City, and I was happy to help. I texted Pat with Doomsday's number and told Pat to work it out with Doomsday. When did this happen? Look at the texts! I can't be expected to remember dates.

Yes, Exhibit 2 shows texts between me and Doomsday. I don't remember what I meant when I asked Doomsday for "c." Maybe I meant vitamin C. Or candy. I mean, what else starts with "c"? It was so long ago.

Doomsday did the negotiating and wrote the contract, as always. I listened to part of one of their calls in November YR-2, because Doomsday put it on speaker while I was napping on the office couch. I find that sort of thing stressful and kind of boring, to be honest, and Doomsday is very protective of me, so I didn't pay much attention. All I remember about the call is Doomsday saying that the terms they discussed would be put into the contract.

I didn't really read the contract, either. I know that if Doomsday is in charge, things will be alright. I did sign the contract electronically. Exhibit 4 is a true and correct copy as far as I know. The gist of it is that I was going to do a concert in February YR-1 and donate the profits to Paradise Partners.

Two days before the concert, I realized that the energy around the concert was toxic. I had been on the road doing concerts for months and I was feeling off, spiritually and physically. I had a runny nose and I was run down. No, no other symptoms. But it was also really cold in Nita City, with freezing temperatures and snow. I knew that my well-being would be in jeopardy if I went there. I have never liked cold weather and it always takes a toll on me. And singing two one-hour sets? That's just too much. I told Doomsday to let Pat know that it was just too cold in Nita City and we couldn't make it to the concert.

I was sorry to disappoint Pat, but as my yoga instructor tells me, you can't pour from an empty cup. I needed to take care of myself before I could take care of anyone else. I know that Doomsday is being criticized for sending me a text that night that said, "One concert is not going to change their pathetic little lives anyway." That was a joke, obviously. That's just Doomsday's sense of humor. Exhibit 10 is a copy of that text.

After making the decision not to go to Nita City, I instantly felt better. I was proud of myself for listening to my need for self-care. I had also been talking to Yummy, the headliner for that year's Super Bowl in Las Vegas, which happened to be scheduled the same day as the charity concert for Paradise Partners. I don't remember exactly when we started discussing it, but a few days before the charity concert, Yummy said maybe I could do a guest appearance at the halftime show, which would have been amazing. Doomsday was excited about it because all those viewers translate into cash. Plus, performing at the Super Bowl meant going to Las Vegas, where it was forecast to be warm and sunny that weekend. From a holistic perspective, it was the right thing to do. I sent word on FriendMe to my fans, "On to LV, my precious Sparklers!!" I've seen a copy of Exhibit 8 and yes, that's the message I sent. I've also seen Exhibit 7, which supposedly shows texts that Pat sent to me. I guess those texts went to my phone, but I really don't remember getting them.

I should have known that Yummy might not follow through with the offer—everyone knows how flaky Yummy is. I don't want to discuss what happened between us because our altercation is nobody's business and I don't want to put negative energy out there. Okay, since you're insisting on an answer, I think Yummy was jealous because I'm getting more popular and Yummy's boo was crushing on me. Whatev. In the end, I did go to Las Vegas but I didn't perform at halftime. C'est la vie.

A few weeks later, Doomsday called me, furious because Pat had made a fake video of me praising Paradise Partners and asking my fans to donate at least $100 or as much as they could. Apparently, they took footage that Doomsday had sent over of me talking about Paradise Partners and asking people to come to the concert, and they changed it so in the video I'm asking for donations instead of asking people to buy tickets. Doomsday forwarded the video to me, and I looked really good! I don't know how that technology works, but it sounds and looks exactly like me. And my Sparklers are the best! They have such big hearts and they would do anything for me. *Paparazzi!* magazine even did a story about how generous I was to have helped Paradise Partners like this. Apparently, my fans donated a lot of money! It looks like Exhibit 17 is the article—I've seen it, but to be honest I don't even remember doing that interview. I talk to a lot of people. I might have said those things. I don't remember what I meant by them.

Doomsday insisted on shutting it down, though. It's always "business first" with Doomsday. I heard Doomsday call Pat. Doomsday told Pat to take down the video because it was supposedly unauthorized. I think Doomsday was going to file a lawsuit too. I didn't really mind about the video, and if it were up to me, I would have let it go. Like I said, I'm a really thoughtful and generous person.

# Deposition of Dakota "Doomsday" Dyer

My name is Dakota Dyer, and I am 43 years old. I was born and raised here in Nita City. I was a decent tennis player in high school, and that's how I picked up the nickname, "Doomsday."

I went to both college and law school at Nita University, where I got my BA in economics in YR-21 and my JD in YR-18. Right out of law school, I went to work for a small, family-owned real estate company called the Eclipse Organization where my job was to handle all the paperwork and accounting. My relationship with the owners—who were crooks—did not end well and I transitioned to work as a talent agent in around YR-14.

First, I represented a guy I knew from law school who had become insanely famous online for doing videos where he taped himself playing video games and making stupid jokes and eating whipped cream out of a can—I kid you not. He was raking in all kinds of cash and getting ad and endorsement deals and he didn't have time to handle all that himself, so I did it for him for a percentage. He introduced me to one of the kids who was in the movie *WhoopDiDo!* who needed an agent, and somehow word got out that I was pretty good at driving hard bargains for kids, and I ended up repping about a dozen of them.

Of course, I knew who D.J. Diamond was because D.J. was already a star. In YR-6, D.J. turned eighteen and was dealing with parents who were idiots and not managing the D.J. brand as well as they could have. D.J. was very naïve and did not know anything about business or about how the real world works. D.J. asked me to take over representation, and I have to say, I've done an amazing job.

Yes, there's a difference between managers and agents. Agents negotiate gigs, usually need to be licensed, and typically represent many clients. Managers aren't licensed, have a limited number of clients, and work on the client's overall career and brand. For D.J., I'm both. Yes, it's legal—Diamond's my only client.

My job duties include all negotiations for D.J., including concert packages, concert merchandise, image licensing, and marketing and sales for the Sparkles products. Managing D.J.'s concert tours is another big responsibility, although I do use a road manager to oversee logistics, and I have accountants and lawyers to take care of other things. I am also familiar with the big picture for every D.J.-related business venture, although I'm not always involved in the details. D.J. has a huge fan base called the Sparklers and believe me, meeting their intense expectations is more than a fulltime job. D.J. has been my only client for about five years now. I get 10 percent of D.J.'s concert proceeds, and a 5 percent cut of D.J.'s earnings from other sources.

I also manage D.J.'s charity portfolio. These days, celebrities have to pick one cause or another or they get accused of being "out of touch." So, I try to make sure that occasionally D.J. has photo ops with rescue animals and whatnot to keep a positive public image.

In November YR-2, sometime after Thanksgiving, I got a text from D.J. wanting to do a charity concert for Paradise Partners. My first reaction was, really? For free? In February? In Nita City?

I was surprised it was going to be in Nita in the winter because D.J. does not like snow. But D.J. really wanted to do it, so I figured it would be good PR. Exhibit 2 is our text exchange.

Later that day, I got a voicemail message from that knucklehead Pat, saying D.J. had agreed to do a two-hour set for their charity event. That surprised me, too, because D.J. likes two-hour sets even less than snow. D.J. never sings for more than forty-five minutes or an hour at most. Don't get me wrong—as the concert headliner, D.J. makes sure that ticketholders have a good time by using cool staging and special effects and by having great intro acts, and once on stage, D.J. gives it all. "Smashes it," as they say. D.J. puts an incredible amount of work into things like set design, costumes, and choreography. But anyone who knows D.J. knows that no way, no how, is D.J. singing for two hours.

I have no idea why D.J. said yes to the concert. I guess Pat and D.J. went to school together when they were kids and D.J. felt some sort of obligation—or pity. I did think that D.J. doing a charity concert for a bunch of poor kids would be good publicity.

After confirming with D.J., I called Pat back to hammer out the terms, and I put the call on speaker so D.J. could hear everything. Our call was on November 29, YR-2. We spoke for maybe five to ten minutes. I had to set Pat straight. I told Pat that, under the contract, D.J. was going to do two one-hour sets (not a two-hour set) for a nominal fee of $100, and we would give the ticket proceeds to fund the camp, less our expenses. We set the concert date for February 12, YR-1—it's the only time D.J. could do it. No warm-up act—too much of a hassle and the focus had to be on D.J. D.J. was going to bring some bandmembers and backup singers to perform some of the hits and songs that we're pushing, but this was not going to be part of D.J.'s "Diamonds are Forever Tour," which has massive staging, lighting, special effects, you name it. Pat didn't respond much to any of this.

Pat did say that Paradise was hiring Concerts-R-Us to do all the "concert stuff," which was good because Pat clearly had no clue what to do. Then Pat started babbling about some problems with an earlier fundraiser and wanting to get the publicity right for this one, so I said I'd send over video footage of D.J. plugging the concert. Did I say Paradise could do anything it wanted with the footage? Absolutely not. If I said anything like that, it was obvious that it was in the context of promoting the concert, not using it for some other purpose. I asked if Pat had any questions, and Pat said no. I said I'd write up the contract and send it to over to sign.

That day and the next, I drafted the contract. I just took the standard form our lawyers used for our regular concerts and made some changes because it was going to be a benefit concert. No need to pay the lawyers on this one—after all, I'm a lawyer and we weren't making money off of this anyway. Exhibit 4 is a copy of the contract.

To make sure that we would be covered if D.J. backed out, I wrote a cancellation provision which read in part: "Diamond further reserves the right to cancel Diamond's performance obligations under this agreement for any reason related to Diamond's mental or physical health, security, or well-being, and in such case shall waive the performance fee but may retain any deposit at

Diamond's sole discretion." The contract did not require a deposit but the part about a deposit is standard language. The other part, about the right to cancel, was definitely not standard language but I feared it might come in handy. I had even told Pat on the phone that D.J. would perform at the concert "unless a better offer comes along." I didn't put that in writing, of course, and I said it jokingly because I didn't want to raise any alarm. Besides, I assumed that since Pat and D.J. have known each other forever, Pat knew that D.J. does what D.J. wants. I don't remember Pat saying anything about losing their job or Paradise Partners losing money if D.J. didn't perform, but it's possible Pat said that.

I sent the contract to Pat on November 30, YR-2 on DocExecute and received a notice that it was signed about fifteen minutes later.

On December 1, YR-2, I talked to Rock at Concerts-R-Us and told him what we needed for D.J. to do the concert.

In December YR-2, I sent Pat the video of D.J., which was similar to what we've used to promote other concerts. The video included one of D.J.'s hits, "Sparkle," and statements like, "I can't wait to see everyone!" and "Hurry and buy your tickets now, they're going fast!" or something like that. Exhibit 19 is a true and correct copy of the video I sent, along with the transcribed text of the video.

I heard that the show sold out minutes after sales went live in early January YR-1. Not surprised. Around the same time, we selected some bandmembers and singers to do the concert with D.J., and Concerts-R-Us made our travel and hotel arrangements. We were ready to go.

Unfortunately, I was right, and D.J. had to back out. Two days before the concert, D.J. was not feeling well and had cold symptoms like a runny nose and being tired. Sure, lots of things can cause those symptoms. No, I've never seen D.J. with any illegal drug. No, I don't know what Diamond meant by "c" in Exhibit 2. You better be careful with your insinuations.

I texted Pat right away that D.J. wouldn't be able to do the concert. Exhibit 6 is my text and Pat's response. Yes, that must have been February 10, YR-1. Looking at my text, I don't know if I meant D.J. had a cold and was physically feeling bad, or if it was too cold in Nita and D.J. was feeling bad about cancelling. Whatever. The truth was that D.J. definitely didn't feel bad about canceling.

Also on February 10, YR-1, Pat called and left a message asking me to call back but I don't think I did. What would be the point? Like I said, D.J. does what D.J. wants.

I fully supported D.J.'s decision not to do the concert because that same weekend D.J. had an opportunity to do a guest appearance at the Super Bowl halftime show, which was headlined by Yummy. "Yummy" is a stupid name, but Yummy is really hot right now and doing the Super Bowl would have brought D.J. a lot of attention and eventually more money, which is what really matters.

No, I've never seen the email from Payton marked as Exhibit 9.

Yes, I texted D.J.: "One concert is not going to change their pathetic little lives anyway." Exhibit 10 is a copy of that text. What, am I supposed to apologize for being honest? That text was supposed to be private anyway. And I was just kidding around.

It ended up that D.J. didn't perform at the Super Bowl. Flight to Vegas, hotel rooms, and Yummy didn't invite D.J. after all. You can't trust anyone these days.

A few days after the concert was supposed to happen, I got a letter from the clown who runs the nonprofit threatening to sue D.J. Plaze didn't come right out and say it but that's what it meant. Exhibit 12 is a copy of the letter. I immediately wrote back explaining why these lame threats weren't going to go anywhere since the contract they signed let D.J. back out. Exhibit 14 is a copy of the letter I wrote. Ok, yeah, I was in a rotten mood and Plaze's letter got me angry. Paradise sued us anyway and did a press release trying to make D.J. look bad. I think they know their lawsuit is a sham, and they're just doing this to get attention and raise money.

After Paradise Partners sued us, it had the nerve to raise money using a deepfake of D.J. On March 25, YR-1—I remember because it's my Doberman's birthday—one of our interns forwarded me a copy of a video that was supposedly D.J. doing a fundraising promo for Paradise Partners. There was one problem—D.J. never did a fundraising promo for Paradise Partners. We figure those thieves at their so-called "nonprofit" manipulated the videos we gave them without our permission and they used that deepfake to get D.J.'s fans to send donations. They can't do that! We own the rights to D.J.'s images, and those images are worth real money. I showed the video to D.J. that same day. D.J. liked it and said it was "fire," whatever that means, but I convinced D.J. that you can't let people make money off your property like that. D.J. eventually agreed to sue Paradise Partners for damages based on the video.

It's true that when I was much younger, I made some mistakes. Without getting into too many details, 15 years ago I pled guilty to felony embezzlement from my former employer at Eclipse. He was a two-bit con man, a supposed real estate developer, a terrible person, and a thief. I served my probation term and am a better person for it. In any event, I was disbarred from the practice of law, and that's when I started working as a talent agent. Yeah, I could petition to get my license reinstated, but I'm not planning to practice, so why bother?

And, yes, I have heard rumors of people accusing me of practicing law without a license. These people are jealous losers who simply do not understand what a successful manager does, and they should mind their own business.

How do I feel about Pat and Payton? Next question. Ok, since you persist. They're dopes. If you're not in the music business, stay out of it. If they'd just asked for a big donation, D.J. probably would have given it to them for a photo op. I still wouldn't have gotten anything out of it, but at least D.J. could have taken a tax deduction. Are we done here?

[ADDITIONAL TESTIMONY IF COUNTERCLAIM HAS BEEN FILED:]

Of course we registered the copyright on the video we gave to Paradise Partners. Well, okay, I didn't apply for the registration with the copyright office until March 27, YR-1, after we saw the video Paradise Partners had made. We also didn't have the registration certificate in our hands when we filed the counterclaim, but I don't think the counterclaim allegations are dishonest. Besides, the copyrights on D.J.'s songs and music videos, which we used to create the video we gave to Paradise Partners, were all registered.

# EXHIBITS

**Exhibit 1**

## 11/28/YR-2 Texts Between Paw and Diamond

Diamond

11/28/YR-2 10:40 a.m.

> Hi D.J., this is Pat! I think I told you I work for this great nonprofit called Paradise Partners. We're raising money to send underprivileged kids to a free camp that will change their lives! We want to put on a concert to benefit the kids. Of course I thought of YOU—the most amazing superstar on the planet! Would you be the Shining Star of the concert and help us provide hope for the children???

11/28/YR-2 11:02 a.m.

Who r u?

> Pat Paw from high school! Hey we can't actually pay you much if anything to perform cuz we need to raise money for the camp and stuff, but the children really need you! And we love you so much, think of all the new Sparklers you'll make!

11:03 a.m.

oh wow how sweet—I ♥ this idea—when where u thnkn

> How about in February? We can do it here in Nita City...

Hold on a sec

11:17 a.m.

Wouldn't miss it for the world! Hit up my manager Doomsday for details n paperwork 555-719-2023

> OMG thank you D.J.!! You're amazing!!

Type a message

**Exhibit 2A**

## 11/28/YR-2 Texts Between Diamond and Dyer

Diamond

11/28/YR-2 11:04

Hey D, a sorta friend ask me 2 do a concert 4 free 4 underprivilege kids in Nita City Feb—I def wanna do it boo! My heart beats 4 em n u kno they ❤ me so much

> Free?? We don't do free. What friend?

Pat Pa I think. Acc crushed on me in middle skl but 2 shy so u know! Now workin 4 somethin that helps bad off kids

But wait wait wait—is that the same time as that ice sculpture party in Ibiza? Sounds so fun too. Lmk

> The wha? Ibiza?

Yeah where that tower is leaning

> You thinking about pisa maybe?

U wanna get pizza?

> ??

Ok so lets do that concert for the kids. lets do it! I'll have them call u, set it up.

Type a message

**Exhibit 2B**

## 11/28/YR-2 Texts Between Diamond and Dyer (cont.)

Diamond

11/28/YR-2 11:04

Free?!... Nita in Feb?

plzzz

Ugh. K.

TY!! And I need more c plz

And a ice sculpture. With ice. frozen NOT melting

Maybe a lion

Lion ice sculpture not a real lion.

Vegi if u get pizza

No just dbl cheese and jalapeno pineapple, that one u get 🔥 thx

D?

Dakota?

Oh Dakota!

DAKOTA!!!!!!!

DAKOTA!!!!!!!!!!!!!!!!!!!!!!!!!!!!!!!!!

Here baby. Got u.

Type a message

**Exhibit 2C**

## 11/28/YR-2 Texts Between Diamond and Dyer (cont.)

**Diamond**

11/28/YR-2 11:04

Ty. Been next door to u in the meditation room all this time, meditating. Its like thinking

I need to start a clothing line

Or shoes

Dakota?

DAKOTA??

**Exhibit 3**

## 11/29/YR-2 Paw's Handwritten Notes from Call with Dyer

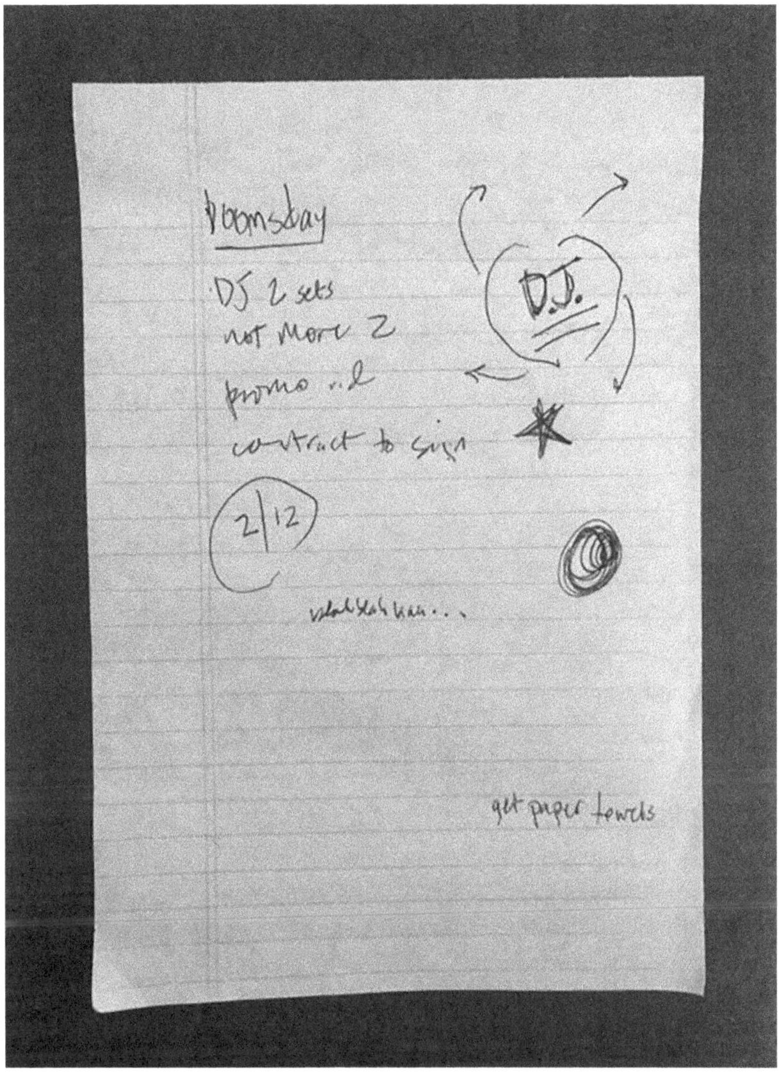

Exhibit 4

# Agreement for Concert Performance

This Agreement for Concert Performance ("agreement") is entered into by D.J. Diamond ("Diamond") and Paradise Partners ("Paradise") as of November 30, YR-2.

**1. SERVICES TO BE PROVIDED BY DIAMOND**

1.1. Diamond shall appear at a concert scheduled by Paradise for February 12, YR-1 ("concert") at a location suitable to performer ("venue") in Nita City, Nita.

1.2. Diamond shall perform songs in two sets. Each set shall last no more than sixty minutes. The first set shall start not earlier than 7:00 p.m. The last set shall end not later than 10:00 p.m.

1.3. It is understood and agreed that the concert, and Diamond's performance at the concert, will not be a part of, or a replication of, any aspect of the *Diamonds are Forever Tour*. The concert will therefore not include all Diamond's musicians, singers, dancers, crew, stage sets, lighting, special effects, costumes, etc. as might otherwise be used on tour. Instead, Paradise will provide the stage and all required equipment (including audio equipment, lighting, sets, and instruments as may be requested) and personnel (including musicians and back-up singers as may be requested), including as set forth herein. Diamond will perform songs of Diamond's choice, which will include some of Diamond's best-selling songs. There will be no warm-up act for this concert without Diamond's express permission upon reasonable notice.

**2. SERVICES TO BE PROVIDED BY PARADISE**

2.1. Paradise shall provide the following, directly or through Concerts-R-Us:

a. The venue for the concert.

b. Permits and licenses required to conduct the concert in compliance with law.

c. Equipment and personnel for the operation of the concert and Diamond's performance, consistent with Diamond's requirements as set forth in the separate "Diamond's Dos and Don'ts for Non-Tour Performances," which is made a part hereof and shall be provided to Paradise's agent, Concerts-R-Us.

d. Advance payment (or reimbursement) for the travel and transportation costs of Diamond, band members selected by Diamond, Diamond's manager, and not more than five others selected by Diamond (guests), at first-class airfare or private car, roundtrip between their residence and the venue.

e. Advance payment (or reimbursement within 14 days of the concert) for hotel accommodations for Diamond and each band member, manager, and any guest, at a hotel that has a rating of not less than 4.5 Yelp stars, 24-hour room service, and sufficient security, for a period of two consecutive nights commencing February 11, YR-1.

f. Food and beverage for Diamond and each band member, manager, and guest as Diamond may reasonably request during a period extending two hours before the concert begins and an hour after Diamond finishes the last set.

g. In lieu of the Diamond's standard tour rider, the following:

i. a dressing room of not less than 400 square feet maintained at 68 degrees F., containing (1) private restroom and bath facilities; (2) nothing blue in color; (3) nothing made of animal skin; (4) one cotton candy machine, with cotton candy (pink, not blue); (5) one case of non-alcoholic champagne, chilled; (6) one case of non-carbonated Perrier, chilled; (7) seven green apples, one of them sliced into sixteen pieces; (8) three bowls, each containing one pound of M&Ms, with the blue ones removed; and

ii. an on-call runner to address the needs of the performer as they might arise.

**3. COMPENSATION FOR DIAMOND'S SERVICES**

3.1. Paradise shall pay Diamond the nominal sum of $100 for services performed under this agreement ("performance fee"). Of this amount, a deposit of $ n/a shall be due within seven days of the date of this agreement. Full payment shall be completed by electronic transfer before the concert on February 12, YR-1.

3.2. Paradise and Diamond understand that the purpose of the concert is to benefit Paradise's not-for-profit activities. Diamond therefore agrees, as to this concert only, that Paradise may retain all revenue it receives from ticket sales, sales of merchandise and food/beverage, parking fees, and other revenue from the concert, except as stated in this agreement.

**4. PROMOTIONAL MATERIAL AND ADVERTISEMENTS**

4.1. Diamond shall provide Paradise with a video to be used for promotion at a reasonable time before the concert date.

4.2. Paradise shall provide Diamond with an advance copy of any other material Paradise plans to use to promote the concert, including electronic and hard copy advertisements, posters, photographs, and video and audio recordings, to ensure that Diamond is not portrayed in an unfavorable light. All such material shall be provided at least seven days before the material is released to the public. Upon Diamond's demand, Paradise shall not publish, shall cease publication, and shall take all reasonable steps to retract and remove any publicity, promotion, or advertisement that Diamond believes is unfavorable to Diamond.

**5. CANCELLATION**

5.1. If Paradise cancels this agreement less than 30 days before the concert date, Paradise shall be responsible for Diamond's fee as stated in paragraph 3 of this agreement, and any costs incurred by Diamond as stated in paragraph 2 of this agreement, unless the cancellation is due to an act of God or closure by any local, state, or federal law.

5.2. If Diamond cancels this agreement or fails to perform at the concert due to an act of God, civil war, natural disaster, or transportation problem, Paradise's obligations under this agreement remain.

5.3. Diamond further reserves the right to cancel Diamond's performance obligations under this agreement for any reason related to Diamond's mental or physical health, security, or well-being, and in such case shall waive the performance fee but may retain any deposit at Diamond's sole discretion.

**6. INDEMNIFICATION**

6.1. Paradise shall indemnify and hold harmless Diamond and Diamond's manager, as well as their employees, agents, successors, and assigns, from any liability to third parties arising out of the concert or arising from any actions or omissions of Paradise or its officers, directors, shareholders, principals, employees, or agents.

**7. ARBITRATION**

In the event of any claim or dispute between the parties arising out of or related to this agreement or the conduct required by the agreement, the parties may submit the matter to binding arbitration rather than a court. However, the party alleging the claim must request arbitration in writing within 30 days after the date of any purported breach or wrongdoing, and the party opposing the claim must file a motion to compel arbitration within 30 days of service of a summons and complaint. A failure to comply with these deadlines shall be considered a waiver of the right to arbitrate. Any arbitration conducted under this paragraph shall be conducted under the then-existing rules of the Nita Arbitration Association.

**8. ATTORNEY FEES**

If any claim or dispute arising out of the provisions of this agreement is submitted to arbitration under paragraph 7 of this agreement or is the subject of a lawsuit in court, the prevailing party shall collect from the other party all costs it incurred in the proceeding, including without limitation reasonable attorney fees.

**9. CHOICE OF LAW**

The agreement is to be governed by and construed in accordance with the laws of the State of Nita, without regard to its principles of conflict of laws.

**10. AUTHORITY TO SIGN**

If an individual signs on behalf of Paradise and/or Diamond below, it is agreed that the signatory is lawfully authorized to enter into this agreement on behalf of such entity.

**11. ENTIRE AGREEMENT / AMENDMENT**

This agreement constitutes the entire agreement and understanding between the parties, and it supersedes any and all preceding oral or written representations. The agreement may be amended only in a writing expressly agreed to by the parties.

Paradise Partners

By Pat Paw: *Pat Paw* __________ (signature)

D.J. Diamond: *D.J. Diamond* __________ (signature)

**Exhibit 5**

## 12/2/YR-2 Concerts-R-Us Letter to Paw Constituting Paradise Partners Contract

CONCERTS-R-US

Pat Paw
Paradise Partners
1777 Paradise Parkway
Nita City, Nita 80027

**Re: Benefit Concert 2/12/YR-1**

Dear Pat,

Thank you for choosing Concerts-R-Us to provide concert promotion services for your benefit concert scheduled February 12, YR-1. This letter summarizes the scope of our services and pricing for this engagement. With your electronic signature on the last page of this letter, it will constitute a binding contract.

**A. Scope of Our Work**

As we discussed, a concert promoter usually books the performing artist(s) and venue (and all related vendors and workers), and does the marketing, sells the tickets, collects the money, and then distributes the funds to the artists and others. Because you have already contracted with D.J. Diamond to be the performing artist, the scope of our engagement is limited to our other services as set forth in this letter.

We understand that pursuant to the "Agreement for Concert Performance" dated November 30, YR-2 (concert contract), Diamond will perform a scaled-down show rather than the usual tour concert. (When on tour, a performer like Diamond may travel with dozens of musicians and crewmembers and many trailer-trucks of equipment and staging.

1 Avenue of the Stars
Nita City, Nita 80027
reply to rock@concertsrus.com

The setup at the concert site takes at least a day.) At this performance, we need only transport Diamond to the venue with key band members, backup singers, and dancers of Diamond's choice, and Diamond will perform two 1-hour sets, including greatest hits. Diamond's manager has provided us with all needs regarding equipment, lighting, crew, sets, musicians, and back-up singers.

The short lead time for this contract is challenging, to say the least. Most promoters would call arranging and promoting a concert by February 12, YR-1 an impossible task. But because of our connections with the 15,000-seat Nita City Amphitheater and local vendors, CRU is up to the challenge. We cannot, however, accommodate further changes to the ticketing, the venue requirements, or transportation.

Diamond is already signed to do a scaled-down show and Diamond's manager has approved the venue. Consider yourself lucky; despite the short notice, I have confirmed the amphitheater for the benefit concert on February 12, YR-1. While the amphitheater was not yet booked, due largely to the Super Bowl taking place on the same day, I used my connections with the facility manager to obtain the discounted price of $20,000 for the concert. I explained your benevolent cause, pointed out the ongoing construction in the east parking lot, and the manager agreed to meet my price.

Upon your execution of this agreement, we will confirm the booking of the facility with a nonrefundable deposit of $10,000 and the balance of $10,000 to be paid by January 1, YR-1. Beginning right away and continuing through the concert date, we will arrange for food and beverage vendors, merchandise vendors, staff (ticket-takers, janitorial, and parking), and security; confirm delivery of all equipment, goods, and personnel Diamond has requested in the concert contract; market the concert; and sell the tickets. As further good news, our marketing avenues have agreed to provide their services at cost in support of your mission. Tickets will go on sale on or about January 2, YR-1.

**B. Ticket Revenue Estimates**

Given Diamond's popularity and the good cause Paradise represents, we anticipate selling all 15,000 tickets. Although dynamic pricing may affect ultimate proceeds, our algorithm estimates that we will sell approximately 1,250 tickets at $575, 5,800 tickets at $250, 6,200 tickets at $125, and 1,750 tickets at $85, which would generate gross ticket revenue of $3,092,500. (Of course, this amount would be reduced to the extent you decide to give tickets away for free.)

Additional ticket-related revenue is generated by a 10 percent ticket processing fee, which is added to the consumer's purchase.* We have contracted for ticket processing with the industry-leader, EventStar. EventStar charges a 3 percent service fee, with the additional 7 percent passing through to the promoter/artist. Based on ticket revenue of $3,092,500, this would yield additional revenue of $216,475, increasing total revenue to $3,308,975.†

* Use of a ticket processing vendor is necessary because the software required to create, process, and distribute tickets is highly specialized. Processing services done in-house would be prohibitively expensive and would ultimately raise the cost of concert tickets or lower the final revenue paid to Paradise Partners.

† As promoter, we reserve the right to make revenue from merchandise and other vendors, which does not affect ticket-based revenue to you. Merchandise revenue may at times be shared by the artist and the venue.

### C. Distribution of Revenue and Payment for Our Costs and Services

You asked how the gross ticket revenue will be distributed. There are variations based on regional differences and the relative bargaining power of the artist, but generally there are two main methods for distributing proceeds from a typical music concert.

Using the first method, after deducting taxes (roughly 5 percent) and license fees paid to performing rights organizations such as ASCAP and BMI ("PRO fees") (roughly 0.8 percent), artists receive 80–90 percent of the gross revenues. From this, artists give their manager/agents a cut and pay "artist costs," such as musicians, singers, sets, stage/lighting, and transportation. The promoter receives the remaining 10–20 percent, from which the promoter pays "concert costs," such as the concert venue, marketing and promotion, security, ushers, vendors, parking, permits, insurance, supplemental stage/sound/lighting, etc.

Using the alternative method, taxes and PRO fees are paid, the artist receives a guaranteed payment (Diamond would likely command as much as $750,000, which would cover artist costs), the concert expenses are paid, and then the remainder is shared by the artist and promoter at an agreed percentage. (Under either method, an artist like Diamond could earn $1 million to $2 million per sold-out show at a 15,000-seat venue.)

For a benefit concert, however, a slightly different distribution structure is appropriate. Essentially, Paradise will receive what the performer would have received (minus the $100 guarantee in this case), less the artist's costs of musicians, staging, lighting, transportation, and the like. Again, this can be accomplished in one of two ways.

One way is to use one of the distribution structures mentioned above for regular concerts, and then the artist donates their share of the revenue, after artist costs, to the recipient. However, Diamond's manager did not agree to do it that way.

The alternative method, which we will follow here given Diamond's demands and the constraints of the concert contract, is to parse out the ticket revenue as follows:*

* Please consult your tax advisor and attorney to assure that the arrangement does not affect your tax-exempt status or yield tax disadvantages. We do not provide tax or legal advice.

| | |
|---|---|
| **Estimated Gross Ticket Revenue*** | **$3,308,975** |
| **Estimated Deductions from Ticket Revenue**† | |
| Taxes—5 percent of gross (based on estimated gross sales) | $165,449 |
| PRO fee (ASCAP/BMI), full cover at 0.8 percent of gross sales | 26,472 |
| Guaranteed payment to artist | 100 |
| Payment to Paradise Partners | 750,000 |
| Concert Expenses (paid from ticket revenue by promoter) | |
| Concert venue (discounted, w/o sound/light) | 20,000 |
| Stage, sound and lighting- suppl to venue/artist | 22,536 |
| Other per concert contract (musicians, singers, dancers, accommodations, travel, etc.) | 35,000 |
| Security, ushers, ticket-takers, parking staff | 10,000 |
| Food and beverage vendors and setup | 10,000 |
| Music festival permit | 1,250 |
| Insurance | 2,500 |
| Limousine service and artist rider requirements | 5,000 |
| Miscellaneous | 0 |
| Marketing and advertising (gratis by sponsor brands) | 0 |
| Total Expenses | 106,286 |
| **Total Deductions from Gross Ticket Revenue** | **$1,048,307** |
| **Net Ticket Revenue** | **2,260,668** |
| **Distribution of Net Revenue** | |
| To Concerts-R-Us (15 percent of net revenue) | 339,100 |
| Additional Payment to Paradise (85 percent of net revenue) | 1,921,568 |

Based on this estimate, Paradise would receive the equivalent of the artist's guarantee, as well as the artist's share of net revenue, for a total approximating **$2,671,568**. Please note that Concerts-R-Us will not be taking a guaranteed portion of the revenue "off the top," given our confidence that Diamond will sell out the show. Instead, we are slated to receive an amount calculated as set forth above, which will likely be approximately $339,100.

### C. Other Provisions

In the unlikely event the benefit concert is canceled and ticket revenue must be refunded entirely, and provided the cancellation was not due to the acts or omissions of Paradise, Paradise shall be liable to Concerts-R-Us only for the following out-of-pocket costs borne by Concerts-R-Us: 1) concert venue, if canceled after the deadline of January 1, YR-1 ($20,000); 2) cancellation fees owed by Concerts-R-Us to third parties ($3,250); 3) the local permit fee advanced by Concerts-R-Us ($1,250); and our cancellation fee for services deemed rendered ($10,000), for a total of $34,500.

* This estimate is not a guarantee of the gross revenue to be received. It is offered only for purposes of planning and analysis of services. Actual gross revenue will depend on tickets sold, tickets given away, and other unforeseen factors.

† This estimate is not a guarantee of the final costs for the concert event. It is offered only for purposes of planning and analysis of services. Actual deductions from the gross ticket revenue will depend on tickets sold, tickets given away, actual costs, and other unforeseen factors.

(Note: If Paradise cancels this contract with us at any time and the concert takes place, or if the concert is canceled due to the fault of Paradise, Paradise will be liable for liquidated damages of $300,000 as a reasonable estimate of what we would have earned under the contract if performed.)

In the event a dispute arises out of or related to this agreement or our services to you, the parties shall arbitrate their dispute with the Nita Arbitration Association, each party to bear their own costs, with a post-arbitration award of costs and attorney fees to the prevailing party. Nita law governs the interpretation of this contract, without regard to its conflict of law provisions. This is the final agreement, superseding all others and any oral or written representations, and may not be amended except in a writing signed by the parties.

Thank you again for allowing Concerts-R-Us to make your concert dreams come true.

Sincerely,

Rock N. Wohl

Agreed December 1, YR-2, in Nita City, Nita, by Pat Paw on behalf of Paradise Partners:

Pat Paw

**Exhibit 6**

## 2/10/YR-1 Text from Dyer Cancelling Diamond's Appearance; Paw's Reply Text

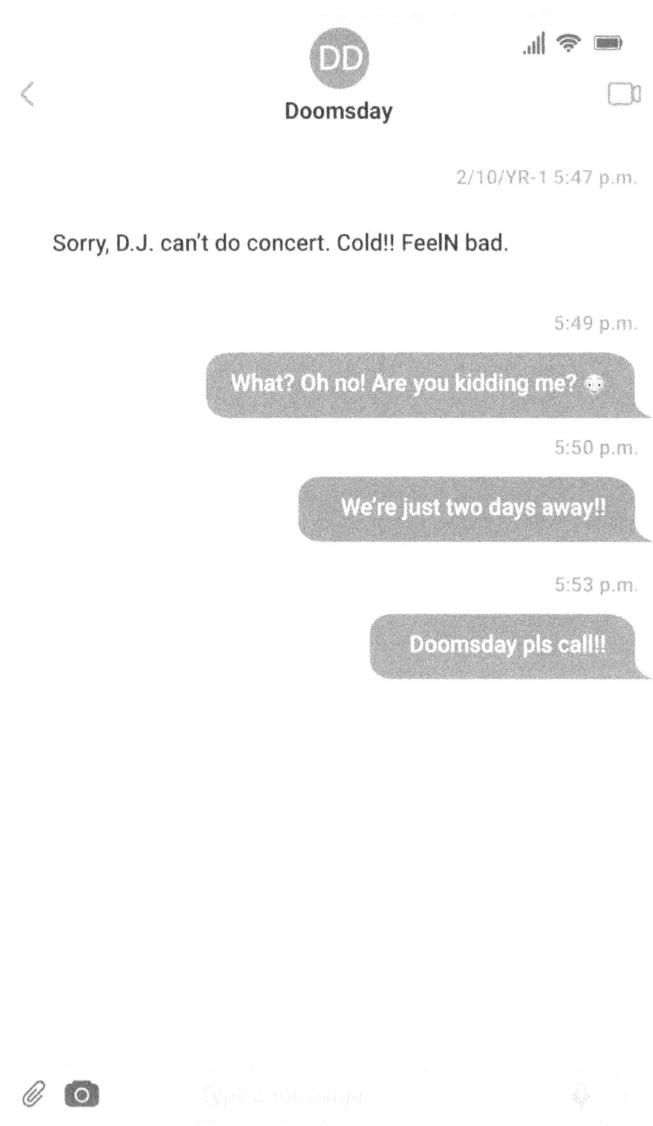

# Exhibit 7

## 2/10/YR-1 Paw's Texts to Diamond re: Cancellation

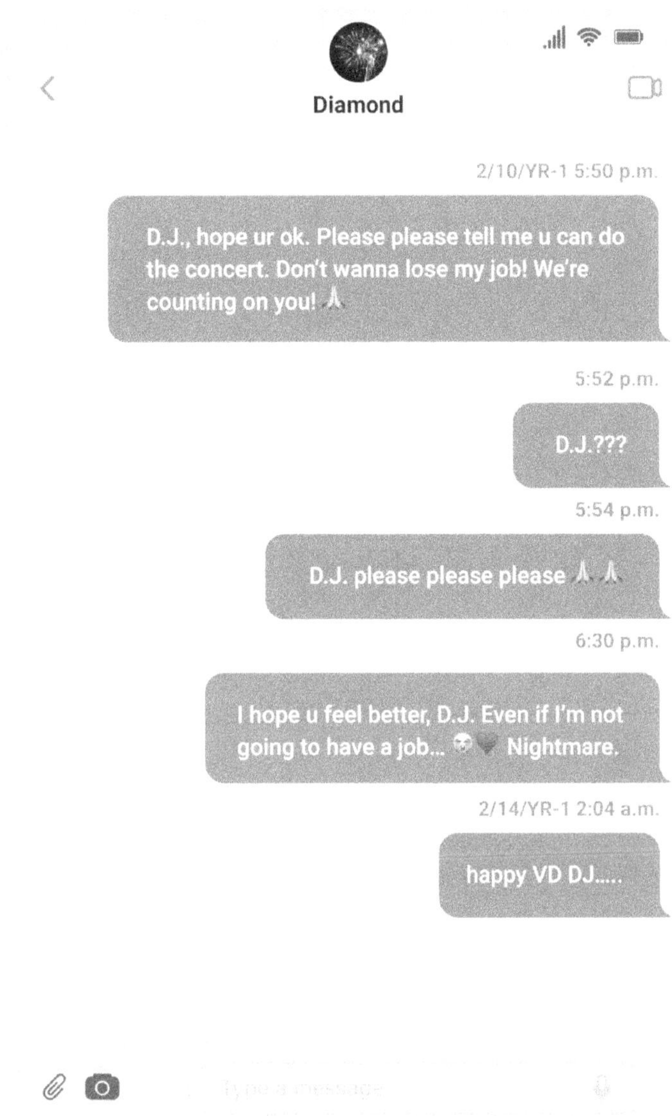

**Exhibit 8**

## 2/10/YR-1 FriendMe Message from Diamond to Fans

**Exhibit 9**

## 2/10/YR-1 Email from Plaze to Dyer

**Payton Plaze**

| | |
|---|---|
| **From:** | <pplaze@paradisepartners.nita> |
| **Sent:** | Feb. 10, YR-1; 7:43pm |
| **To:** | <thedoomsday@djdiamond.nita> |
| **CC:** | <ppaw@paradisepartners.nita> |
| **Subject:** | Benefit Concert |

Dear Mr. Dyer,

I am the Founder and Executive Director of Paradise Partners. As you know, we entered into a contract with D.J. Diamond to appear and perform at our benefit concert, which is completely sold out and scheduled for February 12, YR-1, two days from now. Just today you texted that Diamond is not going to appear due to a cold. Pat Paw and I have attempted to contact you and Diamond repeatedly but we have not received any response.

I have seen a tweet that Diamond is heading for Las Vegas and social media buzz that Diamond will be appearing at the Super Bowl tomorrow. I'm suspicious that Diamond is not in bad health but is simply skipping our benefit concert to appear at the Super Bowl, which will be a breach of our contract.

Please understand that the benefit concert is the only means we have of raising sufficient funds to operate our annual camp for hundreds of children, including high-risk and low-income teens. The benefit concert means millions of dollars to our organization, our mission, and the children.

I implore you to exert your influence on Diamond to perform as originally agreed, so that Diamond may obtain the satisfaction and global fame of supporting our vision for humanity, and so that hundreds of children may participate in our life-changing outpouring of love and guidance. If indeed Diamond is not feeling well, we would make every effort to accommodate Diamond's needs with a shortened performance.

Please be part of our mission. If we do not hear from you by 11:00 a.m. tomorrow, we will be forced to cancel the concert and be forced to consider all appropriate legal remedies.

Respectfully,

Payton

**Exhibit 10**

## 2/10/YR-1 Text from Dyer to Diamond

DD

**Doomsday**

2/10/YR-1 11:57 p.m.

gnite. hey, one concert is not going to
change their pathetic little lives anyway...

**Exhibit 11**

## 2/11/YR-1 Announcement Cancelling Concert

PARADISE
PARTNERS

FOR IMMEDIATE RELEASE

**February 11, YR-1**

With great regret, we must inform you that our Paradise Partners Benefit Concert featuring D.J. Diamond is canceled due to D.J.'s sudden unavailability and circumstances beyond our control. Rest assured that all amounts you paid for your ticket(s) will be refunded to you via your original method of payment. We are deeply disappointed by this turn of events, and we know you are too.

We are in the process of finding additional funding for our annual camp for needy and deserving children. Please visit our website paradisepartners.nita for other ways you might be able to support our mission. Every gift counts.

1777 PARADISE PARKWAY NITA CITY, NITA 80027

**Exhibit 12**

## 2/12/YR-1 Letter from Plaze to Dyer

PARADISE
PARTNERS

Mr. Dakota Dyer
888 Diamond Drive #747
Gladiator Gulch, CA 91506

Re: Diamond's Breach of Contract

Dear Mr. Dyer,

As you know, I am the founder and ED of Paradise Partners. We entered into a contract with your client, D.J. Diamond, for Diamond's appearance and performance at our benefit concert, which was completely sold out and scheduled for today. Yesterday, because of Diamond's February 10 cancellation and your failure to contact us thereafter, we were forced to cancel the concert and refund all ticket proceeds, destroying the dreams of the needy children we represent. In addition, we are obligated to pay our concert promoter, Concerts-R-Us, tens of thousands of dollars.

I understand that Diamond purportedly canceled the performance because of a cold. However, Diamond announced to fans an unscheduled trip to Las Vegas, and I have noticed social media rumors that Diamond will be appearing at the Super Bowl today. It is my concern that Diamond is not in bad health, but simply chose to forego the benefit concert to appear at the Super Bowl, which we consider to be a breach of our contract.

1777 PARADISE PARKWAY NITA CITY, NITA 80027

As I have previously explained, the benefit concert was the only means we had to raise sufficient funds for our annual camp hosting hundreds of children, including high-risk and low-income teens. The benefit concert meant millions of dollars to our organization, our mission, and the children. Please contact me immediately, so that we might amicably resolve this matter and what appears to be Diamond's breach of the contract.

Otherwise, we intend to pursue all appropriate legal remedies and will be forced to disclose to the press and media the unfortunate reasons for the cancellation.

Respectfully,

**Payton Plaze**

Payton Plaze
Executive Director

## 2/13/YR-1 Concerts-R-Us Letter to Plaze re Cancellation

CONCERTS-R-US

Pat Paw
Paradise Partners
1777 Paradise Parkway
Nita City, Nita 80027

Re: Canceled Benefit Concert 2/12/YR-1

Pat,

I was shocked to get your call on February 11 about the cancellation of this concert due to Diamond's inability to perform. It's unfortunate the concert could not be rescheduled. At your request, we will refund all ticket purchasers in full.

Because the concert was canceled one day before it was to be held, Paradise Partners is responsible to Concerts-R-Us for certain amounts. Our agreement states: "In the unlikely event the benefit concert is canceled and ticket revenue must be refunded entirely, and provided the cancellation was not due to the acts or omissions of Paradise, Paradise shall be liable to Concerts-R-Us only for the following out of pocket costs borne by Concerts-R-Us: 1) concert venue, if canceled after the deadline of January 1, YR-1 ($20,000); 2) cancellation fees owed by Concerts-R-Us to third parties ($3,250); 3) the local permit fee advanced by Concerts-R-Us ($1,250); and our cancellation fee for services deemed rendered ($10,000) for a total of $34,500."

The sum of $34,500 is now due and payable.

1 Avenue of the Stars
Nita City, Nita 80027
reply to rock@concertsrus.com

You requested a calculation of what Paradise's profit would be if the concert went forward as planned. Of the 15,000 available seats, 74 were designated as complimentary and 14,926 were sold at ticket prices ranging from $85 to $575, for ticket revenue of $2,918,290. Additional revenue in the form of ticket fees amounted to $204,280.30, increasing total revenue to $3,122,570.30.

As set forth in our previous correspondence, the revenue would have been distributed as follows:

| | |
|---|---|
| **Gross Ticket Revenue:** | **3,122,570.30** |
| **Deductions from Ticket Revenue:** | |
| Taxes = 5 percent of gross | 156,129 |
| PRO fee (ASCAP/BMI), full cover at 0.8 percent of gross sales | 24,981 |
| Guaranteed Payment to Artist | 100 |
| Payment to Paradise | 750,000 |
| Concert Expenses (paid from ticket revenue by promoter) | |
| Concert venue (discounted, w/o sound/light) | 20,000 |
| Stage, sound, and lighting: supply to venue/artist | 22,536 |
| Other per concert contract (musicians, singers, dancers, accommodations, travel, etc.) | 35,000 |
| Security, ushers, ticket-takers, parking staff | 10,000 |
| Food and beverage vendors and setup | 10,000 |
| Music festival permit | 1,250 |
| Insurance | 2,500 |
| Limousine Service and Artist Rider Requirements | 5,000 |
| Miscellaneous ($10,000 budgeted) | 0 |
| Marketing and Advertising (gratis by sponsor brands) | 0 |
| Total Concert Expenses | 106,286 |
| Total Deductions from Ticket Revenue | **1,037,496.00** |
| **Net Ticket Revenue** | **2,085,074.30** |
| **Distribution of Net Revenue** | |
| To Concerts-R-Us (15 percent of net revenue) | 312,761.15 |
| Additional Payment to Paradise (85 percent of net revenue) | 1,772.313.16 |

If the concert had proceeded as scheduled, Paradise would have received the equivalent of the artist's guarantee ($750,000) and the artist's share of net revenue ($1,772.313.16), for a total of **$2,522,313.16.**

Concerts-R-Us will not be receiving the $312,761.15 that it would have received if the concert had gone forward. Please let us know if you will be proceeding with litigation against Diamond.

Sincerely,

*Rock N. Wohl*

**Exhibit 14**

## 2/19/YR-1 Letter from Dyer to Plaze

Dakota Dyer
888 Diamond Drive #747
Gladiator Gulch, NY 10583
thedoomsday@djdiamond.nita

February 19, YR-1

Payton Plaze
Paradise Partners
1777 Paradise Parkway
Nita City, Nita 80027

Plaze,

Are you kidding me?? The contract states as clear as day that D.J. can cancel "for any reason related to the performer's mental or physical health, security, or *well-being*." Did you even read that part of the contract before shooting off your mouth? D.J. couldn't perform at your so-called concert because of D.J.'s WELL-BEING, whether that be physical health or any other reason. Just look at the definition of "well-being" in the dictionary, bozo. And if you don't know how to look it up yourself—which you probably don't—here it is: "the state of being happy, healthy, or prosperous."

So back off, Plaze, or it will be the last battle you ever fight.

Doomsday

**Exhibit 15**

## 3/14/YR-1 Paradise Partners Press Release

PARADISE
PARTNERS

****PRESS RELEASE****
**(Nita City, March 14, YR-1, from Paradise Partners / ED Payton Plaze)**

Today, Paradise Partners, a leading nonprofit organization that brings education, guidance, and hope to disadvantaged and high-risk children, filed a lawsuit against D.J. Diamond for breach of Diamond's contract to perform a concert that would have provided millions of dollars for Paradise's mission and, specifically, its offering of free nature camps to hundreds of needy children. As Paradise's ED, I promise to use every pony we recover to fund our camp and other projects for underprivileged youth.

1777 PARADISE PARKWAY NITA CITY, NITA 80027

[NOTE TO PARTICIPANTS: Any typo in this exhibit is an intended part of the exhibit.]

**Exhibit 16**

## Transcript of *Gossip Grrrl* Snap-Talk Video

I know you guys have seen that video of D.J. Diamond asking you to donate money to that group that sends kids to camp and the after school programs, too. And people are donating money, and that slaps. But the whole thing is a little sus.

Basically, before this video ever even came out D.J. was supposed to do a concert for Paradise Partners, which is the nonprofit. I know, because I've got tickets! Anyway—hold on, let me do my makeup. So, I had my fit, and my girl had her fit, and we looked drip as hell. And we ate and left no crumbs, dude. None!

Okay, so, two days out, D.J. posts, "I'm sick"—that's BS! Because then, the day that the concert was supposed to be, D.J. posts, "See you all at the Super Bowl." So how sick were you, D.J.?

So, then, Paradise sues D.J., and so that's why D.J. makes the donation video—or at least that's what we all thought. Because apparently the video's a deepfake and D.J.'s suing Paradise? Damn! I was like, at least D.J.'s helping out those kids, but Paradise was stealing D.J.'s face? That's big yikes, bro. Like, that's drama and lawyers and [redacted].

But if it does go to trial, D.J.'d have to come to Nita City—and sing on the courthouse steps!

Anyways, Paradise is legit, no cap—my brother shoots hoops there, so if you got the dough, donate to the kids. And I will put the link down below.

# Exhibit 17

## *Paparazzi!* Magazine Article

# D.J. DOES IT AGAIN!

### Need to make lemonade out of lemons?

Ask D.J. Diamond. Diamond was scheduled to headline a charity concert for Paradise Partners, a nonprofit working with children, in February in Nita City. When the event was unexpectedly cancelled, Diamond did not let that stand in the way of raising money for the very worthy cause. D.J. immediately released a video asking their followers to donate as much as they could—and the Sparklers responded, raising close to half a million dollars in the next few days.

D.J. started planning for the concert last fall, at the request of a childhood friend who still lives in Nita City. "I've always been drawn to helping others, especially kids, and when I was asked, I just couldn't say no," D.J. exclusively told *Paparazzi!* "I was really looking forward to it."

The concert was ultimately cancelled for reasons that D.J. is reluctant to discuss, saying "I'm not the kind of person who will drag anyone else through the mud even if the whole thing was their fault." When asked about the suggestion that the video making the rounds was actually not created by D.J. but is a deepfake, and that D.J. is in fact suing the non-profit, D.J. replied, "My manager has told me not to talk about that because there are lawsuits going on. But the bottom line is that those children deserve everyone's help and I like the video." There are no plans for a future concert at present.

14 PAPARRAZZI!

# Exhibit 18

## *CelebWatcher* Website Article

CelebWatcher

ENTERTAINMENT MUSIC LIFESTYLE

### Real Diamond—or Cubic Zirconia?

What is the real reason that D.J. Diamond's February charity concert was cancelled? Is the clip of Diamond asking for donations for the kids a video that the popstar made because of a profound love for the needy? Or is it a deepfake created by others to help the children betrayed by Diamond's cold-hearted decision not to perform? These are the questions at the heart of the D.J. Diamond versus Paradise Partners controversy.

It all began when Paradise Partners asked Diamond to perform a February benefit concert. Paradise Partners offers kids mentoring and counseling, a 24-hour basketball court, and after school programs including a coding class taught by tech millionaire and Paradise Partners founder, Payton Plaze. Diamond agreed to appear, ignoring a well-known aversion to sleet and snow, apparently warmed by the thought of raising funds for needy children. The aversion won out, though, and Diamond claimed to be headed for Vegas instead.

Diamond's PR team insists that they intended to perform at the concert but could not for reasons beyond their control, while Paradise Partners has filed suit, claiming that Diamond broke a promise. Adding to the intrigue: a video of D.J. asking fans to donate to Paradise Partners has found its way onto Duster and other social media sites, resulting in an uptick in donations to the obviously deserving Paradise Partners. Now, despite claiming to like the video and support the cause, Diamond is suing the nonprofit, claiming the video is a deepfake and that the media juggernaut that is D.J. Diamond never agreed to its release.

### Why did D.J get cold feet?

Did D.J. agree to the fundraising video? Only time will tell. Stay tuned and when this case comes to trial, **CelebWatcher** will be there.

**Exhibit 19**

## Transcription of Original Promotional Video

Hi, my Sparklers, it's D.J.! I wanna let you know about my amazing concert I'm doing on February 12 at 7pm at the Nita Amphitheater! It's all for my friends at Paradise Partners, so they can host a camp for needy children this summer. I'll be looking for you there, Sparklers! Sparkle, sparkle!

**Exhibit 20**

## Transcription of AI Video

Hi, my Sparklers, it's D.J.! I wanna let you know about my amazing friends at Paradise Partners and all they do for needy children. Camps. Classes. Counseling. Activities. They're changing lives every day! Now I need you to support them and all they do, okay? Promise? Just go to their website—click "Give" and donate at least $100, or as much as you can. It's all for the children, Sparklers! Sparkle, sparkle!

**Exhibit 21**

### Paradise Partners Revenue and Expenses Summary: YR-4–YR-0

| REVENUE | YR-4 | YR-3 | YR-2 | YR-1 | YR-0 |
|---|---|---|---|---|---|
| Charitable donations and gifts* | 781,663 | 1,286,594 | 1,079,822 | 1,192,827 | 750,000 |
| Grants | 12,000 | 25,000 | 35,000 | 35,000 | 35,000 |
| **Total Revenue** | 793,663 | 1,311,594 | 1,114,822 | 1,227,827 | 785,000 |

*YR-1 charitable donations and gifts amount includes amounts received after Diamond video posted. YR-0 charitable donations and gifts are estimated; includes pledged but unreceived funds.

| EXPENSES | YR-4 | YR-3 | YR-2 | YR-1 | YR-0 |
|---|---|---|---|---|---|
| Camp | 473,000 | 483,000 | 501,133 | 0 | TBD |
| All other expenses** | 972,548 | 1,001,010 | 1,279,540 | 1,340,078 | 1,350,000 |
| **Total Expenses** | 1,445,548 | 1,484,010 | 1,780,673 | 1,340,078 | -- |
| | | | | | |
| **Net Revenue** | (651,885) | (172,416) | (665,851) | (112,251) | -- |

**Includes all other operating costs and total expenses, including without limitation salaries and wages, facilities, utilities, marketing and promotion, supplies, security and maintenance, and professional services. Expenses for YR-0 are estimated.

Certified to be true and correct based on the records of Paradise Partners as of the date prepared.

**Exhibit 22**

# CERTIFICATE OF COPYRIGHT REGISTRATION

This Certificate issued under the seal of the Copyright Office in accordance with title 17, United States Code, attests that registration has been made for the work identified below. The information on this certificate has been made a part of the Copyright Office records.

Register of Copyrights, United States of America

**Registration Number**

**NI 5-046-4782**

**Effective Date of Registration**

March 27, YR-1

**Registration Decision Date**

December 9, YR-1

Title

**Title of Work:** Promotional Video for February 12, YR-1 Concert

Completion/Publication

Year of Completion: YR-1
Date of 1st Publication: December 11, YR-2
Nation of 1st Publication: United States

Author

**Author:** D.J. Diamond
Author created: Video
**Citizen of:** United States

Copyright Claimant

Copyright Claimant: D.J. Diamond
C/O Dakota Dyer
888 Diamond Drive #747
Gladiator Gulch, NY 10583, United States

Rights and Permissions

**Name:** D.J. Diamond
**Email:** sparkle@djdiamond.nita

Certification

**Name:** Dakota Dyer, Esq.
**Date:** March 27, YR-1

Exhibit 23

## REPORT OF DR. PARKER EMORY PEARCE

Dr. Parker Emory Pearce
1824 Skelton Drive
Prospect Hill, CT 06712

Ward, Trujillo & Halgren
1824 W. 54th St., Ste. 2800
Nita City, NI 80019

December 1, YR-1

Dear Ms. Trujillo,

Thank you for the opportunity to evaluate the losses suffered by your client, Paradise Partners. As is outlined in more detail on the attached page, it is my professional opinion that damages total $13,458,010.

This amount is the combination of losses suffered immediately due to the cancellation of the charity concert that had been promised, and losses that will be suffered by Paradise Partners between YR-0 and YR+5 due to the disruption to Paradise Partners' fundraising trajectory. If you have any questions about how I arrived at these amounts, please do not hesitate to call.

An invoice will be submitted to your offices shortly.

Sincerely,

*PE Pearce*

Dr. Parker Emory Pearce

| LOSSES DUE TO CANCELED CONCERT IN YR-01 | Lost concert revenue*<br>Costs paid to Concerts-R-Us<br>Deposit paid to D.J. Diamond<br>**Total Losses** | – $2,022,313<br>– 34,500<br>– 100<br>**– $2,056,913** |
|---|---|---|
| LOSS IN YR-0 | Expected revenues in YR-0 if no breach**: | – $2,685,179 |
| | Actual revenues in YR-0 due to breach: | + 785,000 |
| | Difference between expected and actual revenues: | **– $ 1,900,179** |
| LOSSES BETWEEN YR+1 TO YR+5 | Expected revenue between YR-0 and YR+5 if no breach assuming $2,685,179 in revenue in YR-0 and a 5 percent increase in revenue each year for the next five years: | $15,579,172 |
| | Expected actual revenues after breach between YR-0 and YR+5, assuming 5 percent increase in revenue each year for the next five years: | $4,554,502 |
| | Difference between expected and actual revenues by YR+5 due to breach: | $11,024,671 |
| | $11,024,671 discounted to the present value of money by 5 percent: | **$9,500,893** |
| TOTAL LOSS | Losses in YR-1 | $2,056,913 |
| | Losses in YR-0 | $1,900,179 |
| | Losses between YR+1 and YR+5 | + $9,500,893 |
| | **Total** | **$13,457,985** |

* Offset by donations received in the two weeks following release of D.J. Diamond video

** Calculated as follows: The expected revenues in YR-1 would have been $2,557,313 if no breach ($2,522,313 in lost concert revenue + $35,000 in grants = $2,557,313). An increase of 5 percent the following year would yield $2,685,179 in YR-0.

# Expert Witness Materials

# Deposition of Dylan E. Donahue (Responding to Pearce Report)

My name is Dylan E. Donahue. I have been brought in to respond to Parker Emory Pearce's estimate of losses suffered by Paradise Partners.

I am 54 years old. I was born and raised in Los Angeles and went to college at UCLA. Unfortunately, I was a bit of a late bloomer, educationally. I was always interested in business and finance but did not really take school seriously and wasted my time in college for the first couple of years. At the age of 20, in YR-33, I took a few years off and did a variety of odd jobs in restaurants and retail and even one stint as a police dispatcher, but I finally decided to focus on my education and my future.

In YR-31, I went back to UCLA and worked hard. I developed a particular passion for understanding the markets and got a real high predicting which businesses would succeed or fail in the real world. I made great grades and after I graduated, I landed my dream job as a financial analyst at financial powerhouse Mason Shelly.

From YR-29, when I was 25 years old, to YR-20, when I was 34, I worked absolutely insane hours at Mason Shelly, obsessed with showing my bosses that I was the hardest working, smartest analyst they had ever hired. I read journals and trade magazines constantly, I went to conferences and presented at conferences all the time, and I worked 18-hour days nonstop. It was definitely not a healthy lifestyle and as a result my first marriage failed. I had married my high school sweetheart shortly after graduating from college but after four or five years of never seeing each other, my spouse had had enough. I had tons of money in the bank but I was barely sleeping, my relationship had fallen apart, and I knew that what I was doing wasn't sustainable.

So, in YR-19 I left Mason Shelly and created my first unsuccessful business. It was a graphic design firm that I founded with a former client because in those days websites were pretty terrible and we knew there was a niche that needed to be filled. Unfortunately, neither of us had any experience managing other people, so while our ideas were good, we were not good at operationalizing our vision and we failed pretty quickly.

In YR-17, I started my first successful business, this time on my own. I had always been interested in marketing and believed—correctly, as it turned out—that there was a need for consultants who could help new businesses navigate not just the aspects of business that had always been around, like traditional advertising, but newer areas that took advantage of technology like using dynamic pricing and social media. I know it's hard to remember, but there was a time before platforms like FriendMe and Z, and it took a while before companies understood how to use those avenues to reach potential customers. I called my company OG/NI for "old guard/new ideas" because, the way I saw it, I was going to be able to provide old-fashioned services like market analysis while also using new technologies.

OG/NI took off. Within two years I had 20 employees and within five years, by YR-12, I had 40. I trained each of my employees myself and worked with them closely until they were ready to train a team of their own, which is what made my product scalable. It was thrilling to see the company grow. But eventually I found myself in a similar place to where I had been at Mason Shelly—I was making more money than I had ever thought possible, but I was killing myself, working long hours seven days a week. I had a moment of clarity on my forty-second birthday as I was eating a burrito by myself at my desk that this was not how I wanted to live. I took my time looking for the right buyer and sold the business for a small fortune.

I decided to slow down a bit, bought a house, got married, and committed to spending real time on my relationship. In YR-10, my twins were born. I didn't need to work for the money at that point, and I knew I didn't want to work myself to death, but I was still interested in business and couldn't seem to stay away.

In YR-10, I started my second and third abysmal failures of businesses. One was another marketing firm with an emphasis on artificial intelligence but the concept didn't pan out because the technology just wasn't far enough along to add much to traditional marketing approaches.

The other was a consultancy for HR departments that I called HHR. I was excited about HHR and I was disappointed when it didn't work out. One of the things I've always prided myself on in all my businesses is the way I treat my employees. Not only do I think that paying your employees well and taking an interest in their professional development is the morally right thing to do; it pays off financially. Having happy, well-trained employees who feel respected helps you draw and keep good talent and it makes them more productive. I was hopeful that companies in business and finance would be willing to pay for my expertise in that area, but it turns out that they are not. Too many employees these days just get chewed up and spit out by their employers, which is not good for them and not optimal for the employers.

In any event, by YR-5 I was looking for something interesting to do and started my second successful business selling a computer program called MAPro. MAPro allowed businesses to follow the performance of competitors and compare competing products. I developed it with a friend from college after brainstorming over a beer one night. We thought it would be fun, and it took off because no one else was selling anything like it. I sold my shares in YR-3 and, at the risk of sounding like a jerk, I couldn't think of anything to do with the money. I already had a private plane and a vacation house and a great family that was taken care of.

I had been teaching on and off as an adjunct at NYU since YR-12, and I decided that teaching could be a good way to give back. So, I called the dean of the business school and asked to teach more regularly. Since YR-3, I've been teaching two classes a year, one on marketing and the other on business economics.

My primary source of income now is my podcast, *Market Math*, which is a weekly one-hour show where I discuss current financial events and my personal investment philosophy. Last I checked, I had more than a million followers, which is great.

I am also sometimes a paid speaker. My typical audience would be, for example, the graduating class at the Wharton Business School at Penn or senior partners of an accounting firm on a retreat. In YR-2, I did a TIM Talk for a Silicon Valley audience on how to value a business, called "Prediction is Difficult, Especially about the Future."

Last year, I published a book for popular audiences called *Market Math with Professor Donahue* that, I am happy to say, did quite well and was translated into 28 languages. The book gives my advice on investing and running a business and my philosophy on how money relates to a happy life. This is one of the topics I talk about a lot on my podcast. Money is important because it allows you to do the other things in life that are important, but you can't let the quest for money consume you. The key is to learn the rules of the game, apply them in a way that you can establish yourself and support yourself, and, if you want a family, provide for your family, but then spend your time on the things that are meaningful for you.

My partner would tell you I am still an obsessive financial news junkie. I am constantly reading books and articles about the markets, and I still probably watch way too much financial news. But I think I've found a balance that works for me.

How did I get involved in this case? I was contacted by the attorneys for D.J. Diamond because they saw my TIM Talk. They retained me to evaluate the damages sought by Paradise Partners for breach of contract. I had never been hired to work on a lawsuit, but the work is identical to the work I've done evaluating the value of businesses in the past—both mine and others—and I thought it would be an interesting challenge, so I said yes. I am being paid $1,200 an hour for the time I took to prepare and for my time testifying, and $800 an hour for travel time.

To prepare, I read the deposition transcripts of Payton Plaze, Pat Paw, Dakota Dyer, and D.J. Diamond, and I reviewed all the marked exhibits in this case, including the contract between Paradise Partners and Diamond and the contract between Paradise Partners and Concerts-R-Us. I also read the letter from Dr. Parker Emory Pearce to Diamond's lawyers opining about Diamond's losses, as well as the attached calculations.

Dr. Pearce has concluded that Diamond owes Paradise Partners a total of $13,457,985, and I could not disagree more. There are three reasons why I believe, with all due respect, that Dr. Pearce is completely off base.

First, Dr. Peace's most problematic assumption is that Diamond owes Paradise Partners anything without receiving an offset for the publicity Paradise Partners gained from this whole episode, concert-cancellation notwithstanding.

Dr. Pearce correctly notes that Paradise Partners is, on paper, out $2,056,913 in YR-1. That's the $2,522,313 in lost concert revenue plus $34,500 to Concerts-R-Us plus the $100 paid to Diamond as a deposit, offset by the half million dollars Paradise Partners received because of the deepfake Diamond video.

In YR-1, however, no one had ever heard of Paradise Partners, aside from some charitable foundations that write grants and a handful of Mr. Plaze's wealthy, donating friends. How do I know? Execution of standard electronic research protocols. Yeah, I googled it. But now, as a result of the news coverage of this event, Paradise Partners has been described in all kinds of media. Exhibit 16 is the *Gossip Grrrl* Snap-Talk video transcript, Exhibit 17 is the article from *Paparazzi!* magazine, and Exhibit 18 is the piece that appeared on the *CelebWatcher* website, and these are just a few examples. The scandal has been the subject of stories on television on *Talent Tonight* and *Hello America.* The coverage has included extremely favorable portrayals of Paradise Partners and its summer camp. Payton Plaze was even interviewed for four minutes on *Hello America*. Advertising like that would cost millions of dollars and result in charitable donations of millions more.

And the individual donors who gave in response to the Diamond video are now in Paradise Partners' donor database for future fundraising efforts. Purchasing a list of potential donors who are likely to be interested in your cause can cost tens of thousands of dollars. Simply put, the exposure Paradise Partners has received as a result of one of the world's biggest stars cancelling a concert has been invaluable.

I can't give you a precise value for the donor list that Paradise Partners obtained as a result of the Diamond video because I don't know how many individual donors it contains. Paradise did not provide that information, and it does not appear in the public record. Nor can I put an exact dollar figure on the value of the free advertising. But based on my experience and expertise, I can safely say that the free advertising, plus the charitable contributions due to that publicity, would easily eclipse the loss of donations in YR-1 and subsequent years. Any reasonably competent fundraising team should have been able to convert all that publicity into income. In my opinion, the correct net loss to Paradise Partners in the category that Dr. Pearce has labeled "Losses Due to Canceled Concert in YR-1" should be zero.

Second, Dr. Pearce assumes that but for Diamond's breach of contract, Paradise Partners would have had donation revenues of $2,685,179 in YR-0 and would have received an additional $15,579,172 in donations in the five-year period from YR+1 to YR+5. I agree with Dr. Pearce that the established research shows that a nonprofit can expect to increase its donor base by, on average, approximately 5 percent each year over five years. And I believe that, if Dr. Pearce was correct in using the YR-1 loss as a base year, and if Paradise Partners increased its donor revenue by 5 percent each year from YR-1 to YR+5, Dr. Pearce's math is correct—Paradise Partners would be expected to make approximately $2,685,179 in YR-0 and $15,579,172 over the next five years. I do not quibble with Dr. Pearce's assumption, in the absence of evidence to the contrary, that a 5 percent increase in donor base would equate to a roughly 5 percent increase in donations and donation revenue.

But there are obvious problems with Dr. Pearce's other assumptions underlying their opinion regarding YR-0 to YR+5 losses. Most obviously, it is absurd to assume that, without a breach, Paradise Partners would have raised $2,685,179 in YR-0 and that amount would be the base for successive 5 percent increases over each of the next five years. On the contrary, if there had been no breach, a successful charity concert would have resulted in an unusual one-time spike in donations, with donations thereafter reverting to a lower level of donations and a more normal progression thereafter. Simply put, not every year would be a Diamond concert year. You don't need a PhD in economics to understand this—it's common sense.

Another problem with Dr. Pearce's opinion regarding YR-0 to YR+5 losses is the application of a 5 percent annual increase in donation revenues. Dr. Pearce improperly assumes that Paradise Partners' expected donations would increase between YR-0 and YR+5 at approximately the same rate as an average nonprofit, when there is no reason to make this assumption. On the contrary, if you look at the amount Paradise Partners was receiving in donations since its inception, you see that revenues decreased well before Diamond's alleged breach of contract. This was due to what is, in my opinion, a breathtakingly incompetent fundraising team. As shown by the deposition testimony of Pat Paw and Payton Plaze, there is no one with training, skill, or experience in Paradise Partners' fundraising unit. Paw—who seems to be the sole fundraiser—has made blunder after blunder. It simply does not make sense to assume that Paradise Partners would have steadily increased donation revenue if Diamond had performed the concert, when they had lost donation revenue the year before.

For these reasons, in my opinion the correct net loss to Paradise Partners for the categories that Dr. Parker has labeled "Loss in YR-0" and "Losses Between YR+1 to YR+5" is zero.

Third, Dr. Pearce applies a discount rate of 5 percent to the amount that Dr. Pearce claims will be lost to Paradise Partners over five years, supposedly as a result of Diamond's breach of contract. Dr. Pearce's discount rate is far too low, making the present value calculation of damages far too high.

Accountants use the discount rate to calculate the present value of money that will be received in the future. Sometimes I explain it this way. If you wanted to end up with a certain amount ten years from now, you could invest a lesser amount now, let it earn a return such as interest, and over the course of the next ten years you could see it grow into the amount you need. Think of the discount rate as the interest rate used to determine what you'd have to invest, or the present value, of that future cash. So, for example, $1 put in the bank today at 5 percent interest will be worth $1.63 in 10 years. Therefore, the present value of $1.63 to be received in ten years is $1 today at a 5 percent discount rate. Now remember, the number we choose for the discount rate affects our calculation of the present value. If you invested your money in a riskier enterprise that would pay higher than 5 percent interest, you wouldn't have to invest as much to end up with the same amount. Likewise, if you know the amount you want to end up with in ten years and can put your money into a riskier venture that earns you a higher return, you don't have to invest as much money to reach your goal. In the same way, the higher the discount rate we use, the lower the present value.

Five percent is a conservative discount rate based on government securities and, as Dr. Pearce suggests, it provides a straightforward, transparent method of calculating the present value of the supposed loss to Paradise Partners. The problem is that using this rate fails to adequately account for the risk involved in this case, such as the risk that Paradise Partners closes its doors for any number of reasons. Or the risk that Paradise Partners will continue to do an inept job of fundraising. Even Dr. Pearce, in their text *Forensic Accounting for Nonprofits*, says that the discount rate should be adjusted to take risk into account.

Assuming for the sake of argument that Diamond owes Paradise Partners for the lost future donations that Dr. Pearce claims, I believe that the discount rate that should be used in this case should be at least double the rate used by Dr. Pearce, or 10 percent. This is appropriate if not generous to Paradise Partners, because blue chip stocks have a return rate of 8–12 percent. Using this 10 percent discount rate, the present value of $11,024,671 in lost donations—which, again, I don't believe is realistic—is $8,281,208, not $9,500,893.

Why yes, I am quite familiar with Diamond's music. I consider myself a fan and I took my twins to the *Diamonds are Forever* concert in London last year. I also respect what a brilliant marketer Diamond is. Diamond is wildly popular as the result of some natural talent but also a lot of hard work and business savvy. There's a reason you can't go to any celebrity gossip magazine or website without seeing Diamond all over the place. Diamond doesn't go anywhere without paparazzi following along and snapping pictures. And while Diamond is known as being a bit self-involved, it's in a harmless, goofy way. Diamond may have some narcissistic traits, but the good outweighs the bad. The inability of Paradise Partners to capitalize on this whole episode is inexplicable.

Yes, I have used excerpts from Dr. Pearce's text *Forensic Accounting for Nonprofits* in classes I've taught. I studied Dr. Pearce's work in college, have continued to read their publications, and have the utmost respect for Dr. Pearce. I just think that this is a case where the real world conflicts with dry, academic expectations.

# Dylan E. Donahue

**973 Drenate Avenue, Ste. 4619**
**Sagaponack, NY 11962**

Dylan E. Donahue is a Professor of Economics at New York University and the founder of Market Math Media. The podcast **Market Math with Professor Donahue** has more than one million subscribers, and the book *Market Math with Professor Donahue* has been translated into 28 languages.

Professor Donahue has been an adjunct Professor of Economics since YR-12, teaching:

- Business Economics
- Marketing
- Finance

Professor Donahue was the founder of several firms, including:

- MAPro—providing detailed competitor comparison and market performance data
- HHR—identifying talent-based strategies for recruiting and developing employees in business and finance
- OG/NI—bringing new ideas and technologies to market analysis and advertising

Professor Donahue is a sought-after speaker before professional audiences. Past hosts include:

- Nike
- Chanel
- L'Oreal
- Jo Malone
- Apple

Professor Donahue received a BS in Economics from the University of California, Los Angeles in YR-29.

# Deposition of Dr. Parker Emory Pearce

My name is Dr. Parker Emory Pearce. I am 64 years old. I am a distinguished professor of economics at Yale University. I live in Prospect Hill, Connecticut, with my partner, Alex, and our two golden retrievers. Our three children are grown and we are thrilled that they live nearby so we see our five grandchildren regularly.

I grew up drawn to math and science, and I decided to major in economics in college. I received my bachelor's and master's degrees in economics at the Massachusetts Institute of Technology in YR-46 and YR-44, respectively. I received my PhD in economics from Harvard in YR-41. Immediately after receiving my PhD, I left Boston and began work as a tenure track professor at Johns Hopkins.

After about five years at Johns Hopkins, in YR-36, Yale recruited me to teach and to direct their Institute for Economics and Public Policy. The mission of the institute is to use economic principles to impact pressing economic issues, leading to better-informed policy solutions. We attract research fellows from all over the world who are dedicated to using economic theory to improve lives—for instance, by developing improvements in public health systems or by identifying economic causal factors that lead to war.

I have remained at Yale throughout my career, and became a tenured full professor in YR-31. From YR-21 to YR-15, I reduced my teaching load because I was serving on the staff of the President's Council of Economic Advisors as a senior economist for budget and finance, so I was spending a lot of time in Washington, DC. Nonetheless, I received the title of distinguished professor in YR-9.

In YR-8, I received Yale's Carrol McWayne Chair in Applied Economics. I was deeply grateful to receive this honor, which is given to a professor of economics whose innovative work has made a significant contribution to understanding the markets or trade. The chair comes with approximately $200,000 each year in research funds, allowing me to hire graduate students to assist in my data collection and analysis. I was awarded the chair in recognition of my research into understanding the finances of nonprofit organizations and NGOs.

Since YR-8, I have used most of the additional funds from my endowed chair to continue research in the nonprofit and NGO sphere. For example, between YR-6 and YR-4, I hired a graduate student to work with me with the United Nations Human Rights Commission, helping forecast future expenses in a variety of categories, including vehicle acquisition, vehicle and equipment repair, and the collection and distribution of nonmonetary donations, including food and medical supplies.

At the moment, I am collecting data regarding the impact of inflation on the ability of cross-border NGOs to accurately predict outlays for staff, including recruitment, training and benefits, and physical plant costs over time.

My first several publications and my first book were about macroeconomic policy, and I continue to be interested in the behavior of the whole economy, including inflation, growth and unemployment, dynamics in stock and bond markets, the volatility of exchange rates, the returns to venture capital, and the relation between stock prices and business cycles. But I've always been intrigued by the application of math to practical questions, from simple problems like calculating the odds of winning a round of roulette to more complex calculations like those I've done for NGOs.

My interest in this type of practical problem solving is reflected in a dozen or so articles that I've written, as you see on my CV. I've always been drawn to solving immediate, real-world problems and keep coming back to them; problems such as how to value a business operating in a novel area, like producing a new medical device or vaccine, or how to calculate the present value of money that will be paid at a later date—for example, in a military contract.

This focus on applied economics led me to do the research and writing for my book *Forensic Accounting for Nonprofits*. Why a book aimed specifically at nonprofits? When multi-million or multi-billion-dollar litigation asks economists to provide business evaluations, a multitude of experts are available to provide the calculations for a price, and there are well-established principles going back decades that allow professionals to perform an analysis. There's a lot of money involved, so the research is very well developed.

In the nonprofit sphere, there's relatively less inquiry. So, in YR-20 I embarked on an exploration of the marketing, financing, and valuation of nonprofits. Over the next five or six years I did multiple analyses of how the finances of nonprofits work, and I was published in this area many times in peer-reviewed journals. In YR-18 I published *Forensic Accounting for Nonprofits.* The book got a lot of traction and I'm pleased to say it's cited quite frequently.

The CV I've provided only shows about a quarter of my works. I've edited it over the years to keep it to a manageable length, and this version only includes my most-cited publications.

About ten years ago, a big law firm contacted me to testify regarding the value of a nonprofit here in New Haven. Its facility was destroyed in a fire due to faulty wiring and it subsequently went out of business. It was a sad story. The nonprofit had for many years provided low-cost mental health services to members of the community, and the fire completely wiped them out—this was before anyone was offering services remotely, so they had to have a physical building. The attorneys must have liked my analysis because they hired me in a few more cases over the years to consult or testify as an expert regarding business valuations. Since then, I've been retained on three to five cases per year to do such evaluations. I have always worked on the plaintiff's side. This is only the second time I have been hired to evaluate the value of a nonprofit.

I charge $1,600/hour for my time, whether I'm doing document review, traveling, or testifying. Thus far I have spent eight hours on this case, including testifying here at deposition. The work is interesting to me, and I do it more because of the variety it presents than for the additional income.

I'm here because Paradise Partners hired me to provide an opinion regarding damages suffered as a result of D.J. Diamond's breach of contract. To prepare, I reviewed the deposition transcripts of Payton Plaze, Pat Paw, Dakota Dyer, and D.J. Diamond, and I have reviewed all the marked exhibits in this case, including the contract between Paradise Partners and D.J. Diamond and the contract between Paradise Partners and Concerts-R-Us. I have also reviewed the deposition transcript of Dylan E. Donahue.

It is my expert opinion that Diamond owes Paradise Partners $13,457,985 for the lost profit from concert ticket sales and the costs attendant to the contract with Concerts-R-Us in YR-1, plus current and future lost donations over a five-year period. Exhibit 20 is a true and accurate copy of the letter I sent to Paradise's lawyers containing my expert opinion.

It is beyond dispute that Paradise Partners has lost $2,056,913 as a result of Diamond's breach. This includes the $2,522,313 in ticket revenue, plus $34,500 paid to Concerts-R-Us, plus the $100 paid to Diamond as a deposit. This lost concert revenue is offset by the $500,000 Diamond's fans donated in the two weeks after the concert was canceled.

Paradise Partners' fundraising trajectory has also been harmed and, as a result, Paradise has lost and will lose additional amounts. I calculated these amounts as follows.

Research consistently demonstrates that nonprofit organizations typically expand their donor bases by approximately 5 percent each year over a five-year span. There is robust literature on this point, and I myself have written on the topic. The most-cited authority is a study conducted by Dr. Lisa Chou at Nita State, but The National Philanthropic Trust and other websites provide statistics confirming the trend, as do publications of the Internal Revenue Service.

In YR-1, but for Diamond's breach of contract, Paradise Partners would have raised at least $2,557,313—$2,522,313 in concert revenue and $35,000 in grants. Using $2,557,313 as a base in YR-1, in the current year (YR-0) Paradise Partners should have brought in 5 percent more, which would be $2,685,179. (After all, it is appropriate to assume that Paradise Partners would have continued holding benefit concerts, given the overwhelming ticket sales and the great supply of artists who would want to perform for the cause but would not do so now given the disaster Diamond made it to be.) Instead, what we see is that this year Paradise is essentially back to where it started in YR-4, raising approximately $785,000 in YR-0. So, for YR-0, Paradise Partners is short $1,900,179 as a result of Diamond's breach.

Making matters worse, a loss of donations will continue into the future. Assuming that donations would have increased by 5 percent each year between YR+1 to YR+5, Paradise Partners would have made $15,579,172 if Diamond had performed as promised. Instead, using the actual amount of donations in YR-0 ($785,000) and assuming that donations will increase by 5 percent each year from YR+1 to YR+5, Paradise Partners is likely to receive only $4,554,502. The difference between what Paradise will earn over the next five years ($4,554,502) and what it would have earned but for the breach of contract ($15,579,172) is $11,024,671. Applying a 5 percent discount rate to reduce the loss to present value, the amount of donation revenue that will be lost in years YR+1 through YR+5 in today's dollars is $9,500,893.

I chose a 5 percent discount rate because Paradise Partners is an established enterprise, and there is little uncertainty about its projected growth, according to industry research. Let me explain a bit. In calculating a discount rate for purposes of a business valuation, for example, we often use the WACC (weighted average cost of capital). That is not very useful here, because WACC turns largely on cost of equity and cost of debt, and Paradise Partners has neither, from what I've been told. So, we look instead to company-specific or industry-specific risk profiles and economic conditions, and that leads to the conclusion that Paradise Partners is a relatively low-risk venture and that the discount rate should be somewhere between risk-free rates from government bonds and rates appropriate for blue chip stocks. Five percent is right in that sweet spot. To put it alternatively, if donation revenue is increasing by 5 percent, a 5 percent discount rate is not unreasonable in this case.

I have not calculated the losses to Paradise Partners beyond five years, because limiting losses to this intermediate time frame is a more conservative approach. The longer the time frame, the more speculative. Also, most research into the finances of nonprofits examines five-year spans or shorter and is therefore more reliable than the research looking beyond five years. Again, I wanted to be conservative.

I am aware that Dylan E. Donahue disagrees and, to be honest, I am somewhat surprised. While I applaud Donahue for having started some successful businesses, Donahue's expertise and opinion are not supported by the research. The research in these areas is clear. The 5 percent per year expected growth rate for nonprofits over a five-year time frame is a consistent finding. Based on the facts known to me, there is no reason to believe that Paradise Partners would perform better or worse than the average growth rate.

Regarding Donahue's opinion that Paradise is badly run, Donahue must not know a lot about the world of nonprofits. It is extremely common for nonprofits to be created as passion projects by founders who know little to nothing about budgets and fundraising. The 5 percent expected growth rate is based on studies of hundreds of nonprofits, from the best run, most thoughtfully established organizations, to the fly-by-nights that eventually fail. For all its problems, Paradise is not unusual. In fact, what we see in YR-1 is that Paradise had learned from some of its earlier mistakes and had found a solution to its fundraising problem—hosting a charity concert. In fact, had D.J. Diamond followed through with the promised performance, Paradise would have exceeded the average revenue of a nonprofit by raising far more than what would be expected in its fifth year as compared to its first year.

I am also aware that Donahue disagrees with the 5 percent discount rate that I have used to calculate the present value of Paradise's future losses. Again, I am surprised. Using a 5 percent discount rate based on the expected return of government securities is the industry standard. Yes, a discount rate should reflect risk, as I have said many times in my papers and books. But I believe 5 percent is an appropriate discount rate in this case. And in any event, Donahue suggests doubling the typical 5 percent discount rate to 10 percent, which is just pulling a number out of thin air.

As for Donahue's suggestion that Paradise may have actually benefited from the publicity it received as a result of Diamond's betrayal, I beg to differ. The proof is in the numbers. Paradise is barely bringing in any donations this year, just slightly more than when it started in YR-4. To say that Paradise Partners will actually make money as a result of the scandal around this lawsuit is demonstrably untrue. I stand by my calculations.

No, I am not familiar with D.J. Diamond's work, nor do I follow the *CelebWatcher* website or any other celebrity news magazines or channels. That's not really my cup of tea.

**Dr. Parker Emory Pearce**
**Yale University**
**4225 Gomisnky Way, Building 401**
**New Haven, CT 06520**

---

## PROFESSIONAL EXPERIENCE

Yale University, Professor of Economics since YR-36 (Full Professor YR-33–present; Associate Professor YR-35–YR-33; Assistant Professor YR-36–YR-35)

> Carrol McWayne Chair in Applied Economics, YR-8–present
>
> Distinguished Professor of Economics, YR-9–present
>
> Department of Economics, Chair, YR-28–YR-25 and YR-14–YR-11

Director of the Yale Institute for Economics and Public Policy, YR-36–present

Council of Economic Advisors to the President of the United States, YR-21–YR-15

Johns Hopkins University, Assistant Professor, YR-41–YR-36

## EDUCATION

Harvard University, PhD in Economics, *magna cum laude*, YR-41

Massachusetts Institute of Technology, MA, YR-44

Massachusetts Institute of Technology, BS, YR-46

## SELECTED PUBLICATIONS

"Recruitment, Training and Benefits in Nonprofits: How Inflation Impacts the Bottom Line," *Journal of the Society for the Advancement of Socioeconomic Theory*, January YR-0

"Planes, Trains, and Automobiles: Transportation Budgeting for NGOs," *Journal of the National Professional Economic Association*, December YR-1

"Difficulties with In-Kind Donations: Depreciation and Waste in Nonprofits," *Nonprofit Sector Quarterly*, Spring YR-2

"Revenue Streams for Charitable Organizations: Predictive Models," *Annual Quantitative Economics Review*, YR-2

"Patterns in Charitable Giving Across Neighborhoods and Labor Markets," *Columbia Journal of Economics*, September YR-3

"Economic Development, Market Institutions and Non-Governmental Organizations," *Journal of American Macroeconomics*, March YR-3

"Downwardly Mobile: Economic and Social Mobility in the U.S. and Other High-Inequality Countries," *Journal of the National Professional Economic Association*, November YR-4

"State Infrastructure as a Predictor of NGO Solvency," *Journal of the American Economic Association*, YR-6

"Market Liquidity and the Volatility of Exchange Rates," *Journal of American Macroeconomics,* April YR- 8

"Asset Management for Nonprofit Enterprises," *Oxford University Press*, YR-10

"Government Vehicle Fleets: Forecasting Costs and Planning for Future Acquisitions," *Journal of the American Economic Association*, February YR-11

"Public Entity Transportation Expenses," *Columbia Journal of Economics*, September YR-12

"Nonprofit Business Valuation," A GUIDE TO CONNECTICUT NONPROFIT ORGANIZATIONS, Connecticut Bar Association, YR-12, updated in YR-9, YR-6, and YR-3

"Nonprofit Revenues: Income Streams, Non-Traditional Funding Sources, and Depreciation," *Journal of Economic Research*, May YR-12

"Depreciating Assets in Nonprofits and NGOs," *Nonprofit Sector Quarterly*, Winter YR-13

"Slow and Steady: Returns to Venture Capital in the Wake of a Recession," *Journal of the National Professional Economic Association,* August YR-14

"Bond Markets and the Inelasticity of Interest Rates," *Theoretical Economics,* YR-14

"Liquidity Premiums and the Relationship between Stock Prices and Business Cycles," *Annual Quantitative Economics Review*, YR-15

"Sources of Revenue for Nonprofits: Evolving Trends," *Nonprofit Sector Quarterly*, Autumn YR-17

"What's in a Name? The Intersection of Economics, Nation States and Geopolitics," *Journal of International Economics*, October YR-17

FORENSIC ACCOUNTING FOR NONPROFITS, Cambridge University Press, YR-18, updated in YR-10 and YR-2

"Do Not Pass Go: Option Pricing When Investors Can't Hedge," *Journal of American Macroeconomics*, January YR-19

"When Up is Down: Dynamics in Stock and Bond Markets," *Journal of the National Association of Economists,* May YR-19

UNEMPLOYMENT AND INDUSTRIALIZATION: FROM FARMER TO TEAMSTER, Columbia University Press, YR-38, updated in YR-25, YR-18, YR-10, and YR-5

**PROFESSIONAL ORGANZATIONS**

American Association of Forensic Economics

Global Economics Association

International Association for Business Economics

National Association of Forensic Economics

National Professional Economic Association

Society for the Advancement of Socioeconomic Theory

## AWARDS AND HONORS

LND Award, YR-2, lifetime achievement award for excellence in research and financial writing.

Burick Shanle Award for Academic Excellence in Economics, YR-4, awarded to an economist with exemplary published work and teaching.

A. Colleen French Prize for Economics in Service of the Public, YR-6, presented to an economist who has made an extraordinary contribution to the understanding of public sector economics or finance.

Gilbert Barr Prize in Economics, YR-10, awarded to a financial scientist for a body of work that demonstrates significant original research.

Flaig Medal, YR-15, awarded for the most important and impactful original research for understanding the fundamentals of financial economics published in the last year.

# Jury Instructions

# Preliminary Jury Instructions

**Nita Instruction No. 1.01—Introduction**

You have been selected as jurors in this case and have taken an oath to render your verdict fairly and impartially. Your verdict must be based on the instructions I give you and the facts you determine from the evidence admitted at this trial.

During the trial, we will take recesses. Do not use the recess to talk about the case among yourselves or with anyone else. If anyone attempts to talk with you about the case, immediately report it to the court.

As the trial progresses, keep an open mind. Do not form or express an opinion during the trial and do not reach a conclusion in the case until you have heard all the evidence, the arguments of the attorneys, and the final instructions on the law that the court will give you.

**Nita Instruction No. 1.02—Conduct of the Trial**

The attorneys will have an opportunity to make opening statements. These statements are not evidence and should be considered only as a preview of what the attorneys expect the evidence to be.

After opening statements, the attorneys will present evidence by examining witnesses and introducing exhibits. During these examinations, the attorneys may object to some of the questions or answers. If I sustain the objection, disregard any answer that was given and do not speculate what the answer might have been. If I overrule the objection, do not give the question or the answer any more or less weight than if no objection had been made.

After the witnesses have been examined and all the evidence has been presented, the attorneys will have the opportunity to present closing arguments. Before or after closing arguments, I will instruct you on the law that applies to this case and on how you will go about your deliberations.

During the trial, you may take handwritten notes. Do not allow your notetaking to distract you from observing the witnesses and the trial proceedings. Leave your notes on your chair when you leave for recess and at the end of the day.

Unless in recess, you may not use or refer to your cell phone or any other electronic device. At no time during this trial shall you conduct any research into this case, the underlying facts, the people involved, or the law, whether by internet searches or by any other means. Do not disclose anything about this case to anyone by any means, including social media, except as I will instruct you later in the proceedings.

# Final Jury Instructions

Members of the jury, I will now instruct you on the law applicable to this case.

**Nita Instruction No. 2.01—General Duties**

It is your duty to determine the facts solely from the evidence that has been admitted in this case. You are to apply the law as I instruct you to the facts as you find them, and in this way decide the case.

You must not be governed by sympathy or prejudice for or against any party. Your verdict must be based on the evidence and not on speculation, guess, or conjecture.

You should consider the evidence in the light of your own observations and experiences in life.

What the attorneys say during the trial is not evidence. If the attorneys say anything that is inconsistent with what I instruct you to do, you must follow my instructions.

**Nita Instruction No. 2.02—Credibility of the Witnesses**

You are the sole judges of the credibility of the witnesses and of the weight to be given to the testimony of each witness. In determining the credibility of the witnesses, consider their relationship to the plaintiff or the defendant, their interest, if any, in the outcome of the case, their manner of testifying, their opportunity to observe or acquire knowledge about the facts, their candor, and the extent to which their testimony is supported or contradicted by other credible evidence. You may accept or reject the testimony of a witness in whole or in part.

**Nita Instruction No. 2.03—Burden of Proof**

When I say that a party has the burden to prove an issue by a preponderance of the evidence, or if I say a party must prove something, I mean that the party must prove it by the greater weight of the evidence. A larger number of witnesses testifying to a fact on one side, or a greater quantity of evidence introduced on one side, is not necessarily of greater weight. A single witness may be sufficient to establish a fact.

**Nita Instruction No. 2.04—Deliberations**

After you go to your deliberation room, select a foreperson to facilitate the discussion. After you reach a unanimous decision on each question asked on the verdict form(s), the jury foreperson must sign and date the verdict form(s).

I will now explain the law relevant to the claims in this case.

## BREACH OF CONTRACT

Plaintiff Paradise Partners claims that it entered into a contract with defendant D.J. Diamond, that Diamond breached the contract by failing to perform a concert for Paradise Partners' benefit, and that Diamond's breach caused harm to Paradise Partners for which Diamond should pay. Diamond denies the claim.

To prove that Diamond is liable for breach of contract, Paradise Partners must prove all the following elements by a preponderance of the evidence:

1. Paradise Partners and Diamond entered into a contract;
2. Paradise Partners did all, or substantially all, of the significant things that the contract required it to do or was excused from having to do any omitted thing;
3. Diamond breached the contract by failing to do something that the contract required Diamond to do;
4. Paradise Partners was harmed; and
5. Diamond's breach of contract was a substantial factor in causing Paradise Partners' harm.

To prove the element that the parties entered into a contract, Paradise Partners must prove that:

a. the parties agreed to the contract terms; and

b. each party agreed to give the other party something of value.

When you examine whether the parties agreed to the terms of the contract, ask yourself if a reasonable person in the party's position, given the circumstances, which include the words and conduct of each party, agreed to the terms. You may not consider the parties' hidden intentions.

To prove the element that Diamond breached the contract, Paradise Partners must prove that the words of the contract obligated Diamond to do something and Diamond did not do it. In deciding what the words of a contract mean, you must decide what the parties intended when the contract was created. You may consider the usual and ordinary meaning of the words, as well as the circumstances surrounding the making of the contract.

To prove the element that a breach of contract was a substantial factor in causing Paradise Partners' harm, Paradise Partners must prove that Diamond's breach was more than a slight, trivial, or theoretical factor in producing the harm.

If you find that Paradise Partners has proven all five elements of its breach of contract claim, your verdict on the claim must be for Paradise Partners. If, on the other hand, you find that Paradise Partners has failed to prove one or more of the elements, your verdict on the claim must be for Diamond.

## DAMAGES FOR BREACH OF CONTRACT
## [For trials adjudicating damages.]

If you decide that Paradise Partners has proved its claim against Diamond for breach of contract, you also must decide how much money will reasonably compensate Paradise Partners for the harm caused by the breach. This compensation is called "damages." The purpose of awarding damages is to put Paradise Partners in as good a position as it would have been if Diamond had performed as promised.

To recover damages for any harm, Paradise Partners must prove by a preponderance of the evidence that when the contract was made, both parties knew or could reasonably have foreseen that the harm was likely to occur in the ordinary course of events as a result of the breach of the contract.

In this case, Paradise Partners claims damages for lost profits, reliance damages, and future harm.

**Lost Profits**. To recover damages for lost profits, Paradise Partners must prove by a preponderance of the evidence an amount for which it is reasonably certain Paradise Partners would have earned but for Diamond's breach of the contract.

To decide the amount of damages for lost profits, determine the total amount Paradise Partners would have received if the contract had been performed and then subtract from that amount the costs Paradise Partners would have incurred if the contract had been performed.

**Future Harm—Present Value**. To recover damages for future harm, Paradise Partners must prove by a preponderance of the evidence that the harm is reasonably certain to occur and must prove the amount of those future damages.

The amount of damages for future harm must be reduced to present cash value. This is necessary because money received now will, through investment, grow to a larger amount in the future. Although Paradise Partners must prove the amount of future damages, Diamond must prove the amount by which future damages should be reduced to present cash value.

To find present cash value, determine the amount of money that, if reasonably invested today, will provide Paradise Partners the amount of its future damages. In determining the present cash value of future damages, you may consider expert testimony, if any.

**Reliance Damages**. If you decide that Diamond breached the contract, Paradise Partners may recover the reasonable amount of money that it spent in preparing for contract performance, including amounts that it paid for the concert venue and intended performance of the concert. These amounts are called "reliance damages." Paradise Partners must prove, by a preponderance of the evidence, the amount that it was induced to spend in reasonable reliance on the contract.

**Mitigation**. Paradise Partners is not entitled to recover damages for harm that Diamond proves Paradise Partners could have avoided with reasonable efforts or expenditures. You should consider the reasonableness of Paradise Partners' efforts to avoid harm in light of the circumstances facing it at the time, including its ability to make the efforts or expenditures without undue risk or hardship.

## COPYRIGHT INFRINGEMENT
### [For trials adjudicating Diamond's counterclaim.]

Diamond has brought a counterclaim alleging ownership of a copyright and seeking damages from cross-defendant Paradise Partners for copyright infringement. Paradise Partners denies the claim.

**Copyright Generally**. A copyrighted work can be a literary work, musical work, dramatic work, pantomime, choreographic work, pictorial work, graphic work, sculptural work, motion picture, audiovisual work, sound recording, architectural work, or computer program. The work involved in this trial is known as an audiovisual work, which is protected by copyright laws. Copyright automatically attaches to a work the moment the work is fixed in any tangible medium of expression.

The owner of a copyright has the right to exclude any other person from reproducing, distributing to the public, publicly performing, or publicly displaying the copyrighted work, or preparing derivative works from the copyrighted work, for a specific period of time.

One who causes an original expression from a copyrighted work to be reproduced, publicly distributed, publicly performed, or publicly displayed or uses it to create a derivative work, without authority from the copyright owner and during the term of the copyright, infringes the copyright. The term of the copyright in this case is the life of the author plus 70 years.

A defendant such as Paradise Partners may be vicariously liable for the infringing acts of another in certain circumstances. The parties have stipulated that, if there was infringement by the acts of Payton Plaze, Paradise Partners will be liable for the infringement.

**Diamond's Burden of Proof**. Diamond has the burden of proving by a preponderance of the evidence both of the following:

1. Diamond is the owner of a valid copyright in the audiovisual work; and
2. Paradise Partners infringed the copyright on that work by reproducing, publicly distributing, publicly performing, or publicly displaying an original expression from the copyrighted work, or by creating a derivative work.

If you find that Diamond proved both these elements, your verdict on this claim should be for Diamond, subject to your finding on Paradise Partners' defenses to infringement, discussed below. If, on the other hand, you find that Diamond has failed to prove either of these elements, your verdict on this claim should be for Paradise Partners.

To prove that Diamond is the owner of a valid copyright in the work, Diamond must prove by a preponderance of the evidence that:

a. The work is original; and
b. Diamond is the author or creator of the work or received a transfer of the copyright.

To prove that Paradise Partners reproduced the copyrighted work, Diamond must prove by a preponderance of the evidence that:

a. Paradise Partners admitted that it reproduced (or copied) Diamond's work;

OR

b. Paradise Partners had access to Diamond's copyrighted work; AND there are substantial similarities between Paradise Partners' work and original elements of Diamond's work.

Diamond must also prove by a preponderance of the evidence that Paradise Partners' copying of the copyrighted work was substantial. In determining whether Paradise Partners' copying of the copyrighted work was substantial, you may consider how important the copied portion was to the copyrighted work as a whole.

**Defense to Infringement—Express License**. Paradise Partners contends it is not liable for copyright infringement because Diamond granted it an express license to copy, distribute, and use Diamond's copyrighted work in the parties' agreement. Paradise Partners has the burden of proving by a preponderance of the evidence that it received the express license. If Paradise Partners proves this, the burden shifts to Diamond to show that Paradise Partners' copying, distribution, and use of Diamond's copyrighted work exceeded the scope of the license.

If you find that Paradise Partners has proven that Diamond granted it an express license to copy, distribute, and use the copyrighted work, your verdict should be for Paradise Partners on the copyright infringement claim, unless Diamond proves that Paradise Partners' copying, distribution, and use exceeded the scope of the license. If Diamond proves this, your verdict must be for Diamond.

**Defense to Infringement—Implied License**. Paradise Partners contends it is not liable for copyright infringement because Diamond granted it an implied license to copy, modify, use, and distribute Diamond's copyrighted work in the parties' agreement. Paradise Partners has the burden of proving by a preponderance of the evidence that it received the implied license.

In order to prove that it has an implied license, Paradise Partners must show that Diamond agreed to create a work for Paradise Partners' use, that Diamond made that particular work and delivered it to Paradise Partners; and that Diamond intended for Paradise Partners to copy, modify, use, and distribute Diamond's work for Paradise Partners' fundraising purposes beyond merely promoting the benefit concert. If you find that Paradise Partners has proved by a preponderance of the evidence that Diamond granted it an implied license to copy, modify, and distribute, the copyrighted work for Paradise Partners' fundraising purposes beyond the benefit concert, your verdict should be for Paradise Partners.

**Defense to Infringement—Fair Use.*** One who is not the owner of the copyright may use the copyrighted work in a reasonable way under the circumstances without the consent of the copyright owner. Such use of a copyrighted work is called a fair use. The owner of a copyright cannot prevent others from making fair use of the owner's copyrighted work.

Paradise Partners contends that it made fair use of Diamond's copyrighted work. Paradise Partners has the burden of proving this defense by a preponderance of the evidence.

In determining whether Paradise Partners' use of the copyrighted work was fair, you should consider the following factors:

1. the purpose and character of the use, including whether the copying was done in a transformative way, and whether the use was for a nonprofit educational purpose or for a commercial purpose;

2. the nature of the copyrighted work, including whether the copyrighted work was expressed in the same media and whether it was intended for public distribution;

3. the amount and substantiality of the portion of the copyrighted work used, in relation to the copyrighted work as a whole; and

4. the effect of the use upon the potential market for, or value of, the copyrighted work.

If you find that Paradise Partners proved by a preponderance of the evidence that it made a fair use of Diamond's work, your verdict on the copyright claim should be for Paradise Partners.

**Damages Not at Issue**. The parties have stipulated that the amount of damages for infringement shall not be a part of this trial. You shall not calculate those damages, include them in your calculation of damages for breach of contract, or speculate on what the damages should be.

* This jury instruction sets forth four factors determining fair use. In a deposition program, it will guide participants on potential areas of inquiry. In a trial program, the instruction has alternative uses: (1) given as-is, under the assumption that the Nita jurisdiction holds fair use to be a jury question; (2) in conjunction with a verdict form that requires jurors to make specific factual findings, under the assumption that the court will decide the ultimate legal question of fair use based on the facts found by the jury; or (3) as the foundation for an argument to the court at a bifurcated bench trial or dispositive motion.

# Verdict Forms

**UNITED STATES DISTRICT COURT**
**NORTHERN DISTRICT OF NITA**

| | |
|---|---|
| PARADISE PARTNERS,<br>Plaintiff,<br><br>v.<br><br>D.J. DIAMOND,<br>Defendant. | CV01-123654<br><br>VERDICT<br>[BREACH OF CONTRACT ONLY; DAMAGES TO BE DETERMINED IN A DIFFERENT PROCEEDING] |

We, the jury, render our verdict as follows (select one):

_____ We find in favor of plaintiff Paradise Partners and against defendant Diamond.

_____ We find in favor of defendant Diamond and against plaintiff Paradise Partners.

Signed: ________________
Presiding Juror

Dated: _________________

After [this verdict form has/all verdict forms have] been signed, notify the bailiff that you are ready to present your verdict in the courtroom.

**UNITED STATES DISTRICT COURT**
**NORTHERN DISTRICT OF NITA**

| | |
|---|---|
| PARADISE PARTNERS,<br>Plaintiff,<br><br>v.<br><br>D.J. DIAMOND,<br>Defendant. | CV01-123654<br><br>VERDICT<br>[BREACH OF CONTRACT WITH DAMAGES] |

We, the jury, answer the questions submitted to us as follows:

1. Did Paradise Partners and Diamond enter into a contract?

   ___Yes ___ No

If your answer to Question 1 is yes, answer Question 2. If you answered no, stop here, answer no further questions, and have the presiding juror sign and date this form.

2. Did Paradise Partners do all, or substantially all, of the significant things that the contract required it to do?

   ___Yes ___ No

If your answer to Question 2 is yes, answer Question 4. If your answer to Question 2 was no, answer Question 3.

3. Was Paradise Partners excused from having to do all, or substantially all, of the significant things that the contract required it to do?

   ___Yes ___ No

If your answer to Question 3 is yes, answer Question 4. If you answered no, stop here, answer no further questions, and have the presiding juror sign and date this form.

4. Did Diamond breach the contract?

   ___Yes ___ No

If your answer to Question 4 is yes, answer Question 5. If you answered no, stop here, answer no further questions, and have the presiding juror sign and date this form.

5. Was Paradise Partners harmed by Diamond's breach of contract?

___Yes ___ No

If your answer to Question 5 is yes, answer Question 6. If you answered no, stop here, answer no further questions, and have the presiding juror sign and date this form.

6. What are Paradise Partners' damages?

a. Past economic loss (lost profits, reliance damages) $__________

b. Future economic loss $__________

**c. TOTAL DAMAGES $__________**

Signed: ___________________
Presiding Juror

Dated: ___________________

After [this verdict form has/all verdict forms have] been signed, notify the bailiff that you are ready to present your verdict in the courtroom.

**UNITED STATES DISTRICT COURT**
**NORTHERN DISTRICT OF NITA**

| | |
|---|---|
| PARADISE PARTNERS,<br>Plaintiff,<br><br>v.<br><br>D.J. DIAMOND,<br>Defendant. | CV01-123654<br><br>VERDICT<br>[COPYRIGHT INFRINGEMENT] |

We, the jury, answer the questions submitted to us as follows:

1. Is Diamond the owner of a valid copyright in the audiovisual work?

   ___Yes ___ No

If your answer to Question 1 is yes, answer Question 2. If you answered no, stop here, answer no further questions, and have the presiding juror sign and date this form.

2. Did Paradise Partners infringe the copyright in the audiovisual work by the following (indicate with an "X" all of the following that you unanimously find to apply, if any):

   ___ reproducing

   ___ publicly distributing

   ___ publicly performing

   ___ publicly displaying

   ___ an original expression from the copyrighted work or

   ___ creating a derivative work?

If you answered Question 2 by finding infringement, answer Question 3. If you did not find any infringement, stop here, answer no further questions, and have the presiding juror sign and date this form.

3. Did Diamond grant Paradise Partners an express license to copy, distribute and use Diamond's copyrighted work in the parties' Agreement?

   ___Yes ___ No

If your answer to Question 3 is yes, answer Questions 4, 5, and 6. If you answered no, only answer Question 5.

4. Did Paradise Partners' copying, distribution, and use of Diamond's copyrighted work exceed the scope of the express license?

   ___Yes ___ No

5. Did Diamond grant Paradise Partners an implied license to copy, modify, and distribute Diamond's copyrighted work for Paradise Partners' fundraising purposes, beyond promoting the benefit concert?

   ___Yes ___ No

6. Was Paradise Partners' use of the audiovisual work fair use?

   ___Yes ___ No

Signed: ________________
Presiding Juror

Dated:__________________

After [this verdict form has/all verdict forms have] been signed, notify the bailiff that you are ready to present your verdict in the courtroom.

www.ingramcontent.com/pod-product-compliance
Lightning Source LLC
LaVergne TN
LVHW082343200926
848481LV00012B/3432
*9798886690934*